Bush Theatre

D1630879

RAMONA TELLS JIM

by Sophie Wu

20 September – 21 October 2017
Bush Theatre, London

RAMONA TELLS JIM

by Sophie Wu

Cast
(in order of appearance)

Ramona	**Ruby Bentall**
Jim	**Joe Bannister**
Pocahontas	**Amy Lennox**

Creative Team

Director	**Mel Hillyard**
Designer	**Lucy Sierra**
Lighting Designer	**Rajiv Pattani**
Sound Designer	**Dominic Kennedy**
Movement Director	**Carolina Valdés**
Wardrobe Supervisor	**Natalie Pryce**
Casting Consultant	**Matthew Dewsbury**
Company Stage Manager	**Sophie Sierra**
Assistant Stage Manager	**Luis Henson**

Cast

Ruby Bentall (Ramona)
Ruby's theatre credits include *Britten in Brooklyn* (Wilton's Music Hall); *The Cement Garden* (Heritage Arts Company); *Peter and Alice* (Noël Coward); *Hansel and Gretel*, *Grief*, *The Miracle*, *DNA*, *Shoot/Get Treasure/Repeat* (National Theatre); *Blue Heart Afternoon* (Hampstead); *Remembrance Day* (Royal Court) and *Alice* (Sheffield Crucible). Television credits include *Midsomer Murders*, *Absentia*, *Poldark* series 1, 2 and 3, *Jekyll and Hyde* (ITV); *Blandings II 'Throwing Eggs'*, *The Paradise*, *Larkrise to Candleford*, *The Bill*, *New Tricks*, *Lost in Austen*, *Oliver Twist*, *Doctors*, *You Can Choose Your Friends* and *Holby City* (BBC). Film credits include *Interlude in Prague*, *Bikini Blue*, *Mr Turner*, *Robin Hood*, *The Courageous Heart of Irena Sendler* and *Tormented*.

Joe Bannister (Jim)
Joe's theatre credits include *Wild Honey* (Hampstead); *As You Like It* (National Theatre); *Hobson's Choice* (Vaudeville); *King John* (Rose, Kingston); *Mad World My Masters* (ETT tour/Barbican); *The Witch of Edmonton*, *The Roaring Girl*, *Arden of Faversham* (RSC Roaring Girls season); *Titus Andronicus*, *A Mad World My Masters* (RSC); *Chariots of Fire* (Gielgude/Hampstead); *Bloody Poetry* (Jermyn Street) and *The Lion in Winter* (Theatre Royal Haymarket). His television credits include *Howard's End* (BBC) and *Endeavour* (Mammoth for ITV). His film credits include *The Isle*.

Amy Lennox (Pocahontas)
Amy's theatre credits include Elly in David Bowie's *Lazarus* (King's Cross); Lauren in *Kinky Boots* (Adelphi, London); Cathy in *The Last Five Years* (Lyric, Belfast); Steph in *Tracks* (The Miniaturists, Arcola); Woman in *The Pink Bedroom* (The Hotel Plays, Defibrillator); Princess Pertunia in *Puss in Boots* (Hackney Empire); Doralee Rhodes in *9 to 5 The Musical* (UK tour); Velcro in *Soho Cinders* (Soho); *Decade* (Headlong); Mary Lennox in *The Secret Garden* (Birmingham Rep); Margot and u/s Elle Woods in *Legally Blonde* (original London company); Jenny in *The Prime of Miss Jean Brodie* (Assembly Rooms Edinburgh/Royal & Derngate); Wendy in *Peter Pan* (West Yorkshire Playhouse); Liesl in *The Sound of Music* (London Palladium) and *Sweeney Todd* (Royal Festival Hall). Television credits include Sally McColl in *Shetland Series 4* (ITV) and *Casualty* (BBC). Film credits include Cruz in *Wrong Turn 5* (20th Century Fox); Sophie in *Cab Ride* (Abelle Films Ltd) and Jen in *Never Let Me Go* (DNA Films).

Creative Team

Sophie Wu (Playwright)
Sophie is a well-known actress and a writer for screen and stage. Her one-woman show, *Sophie Wu is Minging, She Looks Like She's Dead*, premiered at the Edinburgh Fringe Festival and transferred to the Soho Theatre. Sophie is under commission from Sky Comedy Drama with an original TV project called *Born Again* and is a graduate of the Bush Theatre's Emerging Writers' Group.

Mel Hillyard (Director)
Mel's directing credits include *Scarlett* (Hampstead); *The Brink* (Orange Tree); *The Late Henry Moss* (Southwark Playhouse); *Love and Information* (The Caird); *Hamlet* (Secret Nuclear Bunker – East 15); *Hard Shoulders* (Latitude Festival); *Even Stillness Breathes Softly Against a Brick Wall* (Theatre503); *In An Instant* (Latitude Festival/Theatre503); *His Face Her Face, Three is Company* (King's Head) and *Loose Ends* (Edinburgh Festival). She has acted as Associate, Assistant or Staff Director at the National Theatre, Royal Shakespeare Company, West End, Hampstead Theatre and Theatre Royal Stratford East.

Mel also works closely with the education departments at the National Theatre and Royal Shakespeare Company. Mel won the JP Morgan Award for directing in 2015 and was Resident Director at the National Theatre Studio.

Lucy Sierra (Designer)
Lucy's recent design credits include *Education, Education, Education* (Wardrobe Ensemble tour); *A Duckie Summer Tea Party* (Hull City of Culture); *Ode to Leeds* (West Yorkshire Playhouse); *Macbeth* (National Theatre); *Young Vic 5* (Young Vic); *Cathy, Benefit, We Are All Misfits* (Cardboard Citizens tour); *The Grand Journey*, (Bombay Sapphire Immersive Experience); *A Kid, This Tuesday* (Arcola); *The Tempest* (Royal & Derngate); *Giving*, (Hampstead); *Another World* (National Theatre); *Calculating Kindness* (CPT); *Snow White & Rose Red* (Rash Dash/Cambridge Arts); *Abyss* (Arcola); *We Have Fallen* (Underbelly); *If You Don't Let Us Dream, We Won't Let You Sleep* (Royal Court); *Sign of The Times* (Theatre Royal Bury); *The Bear* (Improbable tour); *Sweeney Todd, David Copperfield, White Nights* (Octagon Bolton); *Symmetry* (Southwark Playhouse); *Songs Inside* (Gate) and *Fewer Emergencies* (Oxford Playhouse).

Rajiv Pattani (Lighting Designer)
Rajiv graduated from LAMDA in 2014 with qualifications in Stage Management and Technical Theatre, specialising in lighting, sound and AV. Recent design work includes the Bush Theatre's reopening event *Black Lives Black Words* and *Nassim* (Bush/Traverse). Freelance lighting design projects include Tom Stoppard's *On the Razzle* and Nina Raine's *Rabbit* (Pleasance for LAMDA productions); *Blood Wedding* (Bread & Roses); *South Kentish Town* (Arcola for LSDA graduate production); *Might Never Happen* (King's Head & Live at the Zedel for Doll's Eye Theatre Company); *Primadonna* (VAULT Festival), as well as various projects at the Hampstead and the Unicorn. Rajiv was also Production Electrician on *4 Minutes 12 Seconds* at Trafalgar Studios (Studio 2) and is one of the technicians at the Bush Theatre, working with creative teams to realise productions and events in both the Theatre and the Studio.

Dominic Kennedy (Sound Designer)

Dominic is a sound designer and music producer for performance and live events. He has a keen interest in developing new work and implementing sound and music at an early stage in a creative process. Dominic is a graduate from Royal Central School of Speech and Drama where he developed specialist skills in collaborative and devised theatre making, music composition and installation practices. His work often fuses found sound, field recordings, music composition and synthesis. Recent design credits include *With a Little bit of Luck* (Paines Plough); *Gap in the Light*, *Run* (Engineer); *Broken Biscuits*, *Growth*, *Love, Lies and Taxidermy* (Paines Plough); *Dancing Bear, Dancing Bear* (Gameshow); *ONO* (Jamie Wood) and *The Devil Speaks True* (Goat & Monkey).

Carolina Valdés (Movement Director)

Carolina is Co-Artistic Director of Theatre O. She trained at the École Internationale de Théâtre Jacques Lecoq in Paris and at the Col.legi de Teatre in Barcelona. As a movement director her credits include *The Tempest* (Donmar as Associate); *Opera for an Unknown Woman* (Wales Millenium Centre); *The Brink* (Orange Tree); *Treasure Island* (National Theatre, as Creative Associate); *Hamlet* (RSC); *Julius Caesar* (Donmar, as Associate); *Napoli* Millionaria (Central School of Speech and Drama); *The Resistible Rise of Arturo Ui* (Liverpool Playhouse); *Absurdia* (Donmar Warehouse). Acting credits include *Henry IV*, *Julius Caesar* (Donmar Warehouse); *The Late Henry Moss* (Southwark Playhouse); *The Secret Agent* (Theatre O); *The Thirteen Midnight Challenges of Angelus Diablo* (RSC); *Delirium* (Theatre O at the Barbican/ Abbey, Dublin); *Casanova* (Told by an Idiot at the Lyric Hammersmith); *Lindy's Got a Gun* (Enda Walsh at Trafalgar Studios); *Astronaut* (Theatre O at the Barbican); *The Barber of Seville*, *Carmen* (Opera 21); *The Argument and 3 Dark Tales* (Theatre O at the Barbican/international tour); *Bond* (Theatre O). Film credits include *At The Threshold* (Daria Martin); *A Little Chaos* (Alan Rickman); *Call the Midwife* (BBC). Directing credits include *Reykjavik and The Garden* (Shams); *All Mapped Out* (Gogolia); *The Barber of Seville*, *Carmen* (Opera 21).

Bush Theatre

Bush Theatre

We make theatre for London. Now.

The Bush is a world-famous home for new plays and an internationally renowned champion of playwrights. We discover, nurture and produce the best new writers from the widest range of backgrounds from our home in a distinctive corner of west London.

The Bush has won over 100 awards and developed an enviable reputation for touring its acclaimed productions nationally and internationally.

We are excited by exceptional new voices, stories and perspectives – particularly those with contemporary bite which reflect the vibrancy of British culture now.

Located in the newly renovated old library on Uxbridge Road in the heart of Shepherd's Bush, the theatre houses two performance spaces, a rehearsal room and the lively Library Bar.

bushtheatre.co.uk

THANK YOU
TO OUR SUPPORTERS

The Bush Theatre would like to thank all its supporters whose valuable contributions have helped us to create a platform for our future and to promote the highest quality new writing, develop the next generation of creative talent and lead innovative community engagement work.

LONE STAR

Gianni Alen-Buckley
Michael Alen-Buckley
Rafael & Anne-Helene Biosse
Duplan
Garvin & Steffanie Brown
Alice Findlay
Miles Morland

HANDFUL OF STARS

Dawn & Gary Baker
Sofia Barattieri
Martin Bartle
Charlie Bigham
Judy Bollinger
Richard & Lucille Briance
Clive & Helena Butler
Clare & Chris Clark
Clyde Cooper
Zarina Funk
Richard & Jane Gordon
Vera Monotti Graziadei
Madeleine Hodgkin
Priscilla John
Simon & Katherine Johnson
Philippa Seal & Philip Jones QC
V&F Lukey
Georgia Oetker
Philip & Biddy Percival
Joana & Henrik Schliemann
Clare Rich
Lesley Hill & Russ Shaw
Team Nelson
and one anonymous donor.

RISING STARS

ACT IV
Nicholas Alt
Mark Bentley
David Brooks
Catharine Browne
Matthew Byam Shaw
Jennifer Caruso Viall
Tim & Andrea Clark
Sarah Clarke
Claude & Susie Cochin de Billy
Lois Cox
Matthew Cushen
Andrew & Amanda Duncan
Natalie Fellowes & Simon
Gresham Jones
Lady Antonia Fraser
Jack Gordon & Kate Lacy
Hugh & Sarah Grootenhuis
Thea Guest

RISING STARS CONTINUED

Ann & Ravi Joseph
Davina & Malcolm Judelson
Cathy & Paul Kafka
Miggy Littlejohns
Isabella Macpherson
Liz & Luke Mayhew
Michael McCoy
Judith Mellor
Caro Millington
Mark & Anne Paterson
Pippa Prain
Barbara Prideaux
Emily Reeve
Renske & Marion
Sarah Richards
Sophie Silocchi
Susie Saville Sneath
Saleem & Alexandra Siddiqi
Brian Smith
Nick Starr
Peter Tausig
Lady Marina Vaizey
Guy Vincent & Sarah Mitchell
Amanda Waggott
Alison Winter
and three anonymous donors.

SPONSORS & SUPPORTERS

AKA
Alen-Buckley LLP
Gianni & Michael Alen-Buckley
Jeremy Attard Manche
Bill & Judy Bollinger
Edward Bonham Carter
Martin Bowley
Duke & Duchess of Buccleuch
The Hon Mrs Louise Burness
Sir Charles & Lady Isabella Burrell
Philip & Tita Byrne
CHK Charities Limited
Peppe & Quentin Ciardi
Joanna & Hadyn Cunningham
Leo & Grega Daly
Patrick & Mairead Flaherty
Sue Fletcher
The Hon Sir Rocco Forte
The Hon Portia Forte
Mark Franklin
The Gatsby Charitable Foundation
The Right Hon Piers Gibson
Farid & Emille Gragour
Victoria Gray
John Gordon
Vivienne Guinness
Melanie Hall

SPONSORS & SUPPORTERS CONTINUED

The Headley Trust
Brian Heyworth
Lesley Hill & Russ Shaw
Madeleine Hodgkin
Michael Holland & Denise
O'Donoghue
Charles Holloway
Graham & Amanda Hutton
James Gorst Architects Ltd.
Simon & Katherine Johnson
Tarek & Diala Khlat
Bernard Lambilliotte
Marion Lloyd
The Lord Forte Foundation
Peter & Bettina Mallinson
Mahoro Charitable Trust
James Christopher Miller
Mitsui Fodosan (U.K.) Ltd
Alfred Munkenbeck III
Nick Hern Books
Georgia Oetker
RAB Capital
Kevin Pakenham
Sir Howard Panter
Joanna Prior
Josie Rourke
Lady Susie Sainsbury
Barry Serjent
Tim & Catherine Score
Search Foundation
Richard Sharp
Susie Simkins
Edward Snape & Marilyn Eardley
Michael & Sarah Spencer
Stanhope PLC
Ross Turner
The Syder Foundation
van Tulleken Family
Johnny & Dione Verulam
Robert & Felicity Waley-Cohen
Westfield London
Elizabeth Wigoder
Phillip Wooller
Danny Wyler
and three anonymous donors.

TRUSTS AND FOUNDATIONS

The Andrew Lloyd Webber
Foundation
The Bruce Wake Charitable Trust
The City Bridge Trust
Cockayne—Grants for the Arts
The John S Cohen Foundation
The Daisy Trust
The Equity Charitable Trust

TRUSTS AND FOUNDATIONS CONTINUED

Eranda Rothschild Foundation
Esmée Fairbairn Foundation
Fidelio Charitable Trust
Foyle Foundation
Garfield Weston Foundation
Garrick Charitable Trust
The Harold Hyam Wingate
Foundation
Hammersmith United Charities
Heritage of London Trust
The Idlewild Trust
John Lyon's Charity
The J Paul Getty Jnr Charitable Trust
The John Thaw Foundation
The Leche Trust
The Leverhulme Trust
The London Community Foundation
Margaret Guido's Charitable Trust
The Martin Bowley Charitable Trust
The Monument Trust
Paul Hamlyn Foundation
Pilgrim Trust
The Theatres Trust
Viridor Credits
The Williams Charitable Trust
Western Riverside Environmental
Fund
The Wolfson Foundation
and one anonymous donor.

CORPORATE SPONSORS & MEMBERS

The Agency (London) Ltd
Dorsett Shepherds Bush
Drama Centre London
The Groucho Club
THE HOXTON

PUBLIC FUNDING

If you are interested in finding out how to be involved, please visit the 'Support Us' section of bushtheatre.co.uk or email **development@bushtheatre.co.uk** or call **020 8743 3584**

RAMONA TELLS JIM

Sophie Wu

Characters

RAMONA, *sixteen and thirty-one, English*
JIM, *seventeen and thirty-two, Scottish*
POCAHONTAS, *nineteen, Scottish*

The play takes place in the town of Mallaig on the west coast of
Scotland in 1998 and 2013.

*This text went to press before the end of rehearsals and so may
differ slightly from the play as performed.*

Prologue

1998. The sound of waves. RAMONA *(sixteen) stands alone onstage. It is moonlit and ethereal.*

RAMONA *(dramatic).* I am not asleep. Nor am I really awake. I am in that pleasant state in between, immersed in a semi-erotic lucid dream. I am standing on the shores of a small shingle bay. A giant silver orb, otherwise known as the moon, is casting a mystical glow upon this mellow scene. I gaze out at the waveless water for some time, the air is still and it is utterly silent, then very slowly the surface of the sea begins to ripple. A head emerges from it – a boy with piercing green eyes. He stares right through me and it sends a tingling sensation into the very depths of my loins. He is swimming towards me and, as he does so, I look down and discover that I am possessed of a pair of simply enormous breasts which are being restrained only by a clam-shell bikini. The boy reaches the fringes of the beach and, as he rises from the water, hauling himself onto the shingle with two muscular arms, I emit a stifled gasp – *(Gasps.)* for instead of legs he has the oily black tail of a seal. His torso, however – is *all man.* He is a selkie. *(Echo.)* 'Hello, boy.' My voice is rich and caramel and echoes poetically.

JIM *(echo).* Hello, girl.

RAMONA. His voice also echoes – although not quite so rich and caramel. Using my semi-conscious mind I will him to shed his tail. The tail drops to the floor into a shiny, black puddle, and to my delight he is clad only in a pair of tiny Calvin Klein briefs. He walks towards me – sinewy and pale and powerful – and I reach out to fondle his prominent pectorals. But as my fingers hover towards him, I am all of a sudden violently sucked into the shingle. Spiralling down and down. As I spiral, I reach out, and snatch his seal skin before I am enveloped. I scream. A horrible scream that reverberates through the entire universe. Everything is black.

One

1998.

The beach. Night. JIM *(seventeen) stands very still, looking straight ahead. He has blood on his face and hands. A few beats.* RAMONA *(sixteen) suddenly runs on, out of breath. She stops when she sees him.*

RAMONA. Oh dear.

Beat.

JIM. What?

RAMONA. You've got…

JIM. What?

RAMONA. On your face. There's like… quite a lot of… blood. On your face.

JIM touches his face. Looks blankly at the blood on his hand. He doesn't react.

Are you worried?

JIM. No. Are you worried?

RAMONA. No.

JIM. Cool.

Beat.

RAMONA. So. What um… What exactly did you… What did you do to him?

JIM. Doesn't matter.

RAMONA. Okay. That's fine. That's okay. That's fine. That's totally fine.

Beat.

JIM. But it was the right thing to do, wasn't it?

RAMONA. Oh yes. Absolutely.

JIM. Good.

RAMONA. Absolutely yes.

JIM. Good.

RAMONA. I mean, I don't know exactly what you did. But in theory, yes. Absolutely fine.

JIM. Cool.

RAMONA. Cool.

JIM. Cool.

RAMONA. Good.

JIM. Good.

    Beat.

    I like you, Ramona. Even though you're massively flawed.

RAMONA. I like you too. Even though I also think you're massively flawed.

JIM. Brilliant.

RAMONA. Cool.

JIM. Yeah.

Two

2013.

Fifteen years later.

JIM*'s flat. Lunchtime. The lights come on to reveal a small, dark sitting room. The walls are lined with shelves of jars containing specimens in formaldehyde. A hermit crab, a starfish, a jellyfish, a langoustine, etc.... JIM (now thirty-two, downtrodden and wearing a tatty duffel coat) and* POCAHONTAS *(nineteen, aggressive, wearing lots of make-up and a supermarket uniform) enter.* POCAHONTAS *stops dead in her tracks and surveys her surroundings. She looks absolutely gutted.*

POCAHONTAS. Oh.

JIM. What?

POCAHONTAS. Hmm. Okay.

JIM. What?

POCAHONTAS. No nothing.

JIM. What is it?

POCAHONTAS. Honestly it's nothing. It's fine. (*Beat.*) I mean... Yeah no it's... fine.

JIM. Jesus! What?

POCAHONTAS. Well, it's an absolute shithole, Jim, isn't it?

JIM *looks amused.*

JIM. I like it.

POCAHONTAS. You like it? Are you deaf, dumb and blind?! No. I'm kidding. I'm kidding... But seriously, just out of interest, how many square foot is it?

JIM. Four hundred and fifty-ish?

POCAHONTAS. Oh my fucking god it's *tiny*! I am a lady, Jim. Ladies get... plunged in mansions in like... four-poster beds or jacuzzis not squalid dungeons. I mean really – I had you down at least as a more of a 'duplex apartment' kind of man if I'm being honest.

JIM. What gave you that impression?

POCAHONTAS. Hope, I suppose. Blind hope? My actual rabbit has a bigger house than this.

JIM. I didn't know you had a rabbit.

POCAHONTAS. Yes you did.

JIM. I didn't.

POCAHONTAS. You did.

JIM. Genuinely didn't.

POCAHONTAS. Took her from someone's back garden, there's a whiff in here – have you got damp?

JIM. You stole a pet rabbit?

POCAHONTAS. Yeah. Have you got damp?

JIM. You shouldn't do that.

POCAHONTAS. Seriously it stinks like death in here, she's dead cute, Jim – white with black spots, fucking loves Peperamis.

JIM. You can't feed it Peperamis –

POCAHONTAS. I have to hide her though because my mum hates animals and she said if I ever brought one into the house she'd microwave it.

JIM. Did she really say that?

POCAHONTAS. I hate my mum, she's a fucking slag. I wish she was dead. I wish she would just die in some horrible, painful accident. (*Full of rage*.) Absolute slut!

JIM. Okay. That's okay. Deep breaths.

POCAHONTAS *takes a deep breath and exhales*.

POCAHONTAS. There's a right whiff in here, you know. Definitely smells of damp. Or death. There's no way I can live in a damp environment that smells of death – it's bad for your lungs. And morale.

JIM (*alarmed*). Live?

POCAHONTAS. Yes, live, Jim.

JIM. What, here?

POCAHONTAS. I'll get jaundice or that foot-rot thing. What's that foot-rot thing where your feet fall off?

JIM. Trench foot. My flat will not give you trench foot. What do you mean, live?

POCAHONTAS *suddenly notices* JIM's *jars of specimens.*

POCAHONTAS. Oh my god. Is this your sea-monster collection?

JIM. This is my West Coast crustacea collection yes.

POCAHONTAS. Seriously you're taking *these* to Frankfurt instead of me?

JIM. Correct.

POCAHONTAS. I cannot believe you are going to Frankfurt without me. I've always wanted to go to Frankfurt. I love Frankfurt.

JIM. Do you even know where Frankfurt is?

POCAHONTAS. Not the point. You're going on a mini-break with a bunch of bug corpses in jars of water instead of me. That is weird, Jim. That is seriously weird.

JIM. It's not a mini-break, it's a convention. They are not bugs, they are crustacea. And it's not water, it's formaldehyde.

POCAHONTAS (*thrilled*). Formaldehyde? Like date rape? Oh my god. Are you going to date-rape me?

JIM. No.

POCAHONTAS. Shame.

JIM *approaches her.* POCAHONTAS *swerves and points at a jar.*

(*Indicating the hermit crab.*) What's that one?

JIM. A decapod crustacean. Aka a hermit crab.

POCAHONTAS. Why have you got all these for anyway? It's creepy. It's really fucking creepy actually. Having all this dead shit in jars. You're like a body collector...

JIM. Don't really think of them as dead. More... suspended in time.

POCAHONTAS. They're dead. Can't you see when something's dead?

POCAHONTAS *grabs one*.

JIM. Don't touch them! (*Beat*.) Sorry.

POCAHONTAS *is suddenly genuinely vulnerable. She covers her ears*.

POCAHONTAS. Don't shout at me, Jim! It makes me feel really sad! I don't like it when people shout at me!

JIM. I know. I know you don't. I'm sorry. Sshh.

JIM *and* POCAHONTAS *embrace for a few beats*.

POCAHONTAS. I love you.

Beat.

JIM. Mm.

POCAHONTAS. What?

JIM. Mm. You smell so nice.

POCAHONTAS. Do you love me?

JIM. Hair smells of coconuts.

POCAHONTAS *pulls away from the embrace*.

POCAHONTAS. You haven't answered my question, you fucking turd.

JIM. Uh-huh.

POCAHONTAS. Do you love me?

JIM. Well, we haven't really known each other very long.

POCAHONTAS. We have. We've known each other for one week shy of six months.

JIM. Yes.

POCAHONTAS *suddenly strides to the other side of the room*.

POCAHONTAS. Oh did I mention, Jim? I'm going to be a mortgage adviser.

JIM. A mortgage adviser? Ideal.

POCAHONTAS. Let's be honest, I'm wasted as a chilled-food stockist and I've just applied for a lovely wee position going at the Halifax Bank of Scotland.

JIM. Have you got the qualifications?

POCAHONTAS. No. Lied. Said I went to Cambridge and have a degree in Pure Mathematics.

JIM. Of course you did. Is that a good idea?

POCAHONTAS. I think it's probably the best idea I've ever had. I'm going to start wearing a trouser suit and carry a laptop with me at all times and eat those Mediterranean wraps from Boots on my lunch break. I'd thrive in an office environment. Got an interview on Thursday. I'll blow them away. And when I do and I get the job I'm going to start saving up for a holiday in Spain. Have you heard of Spain, Jim?

JIM. Spain? No, no I've never heard of Spain before.

POCAHONTAS. Already been to a travel agent. I've never been abroad or on a plane or eaten a prawn or got sunburn. Can you imagine, Jim? Imagine me, a businesswoman, holidaying in Spain with a sunburn and wearing a trouser suit?

JIM. Oh I'm imagining it right now.

POCAHONTAS. I'm nineteen, Jim, I'm not going to spend the rest of my life sharing a room with my pig-thick mong brother and a stolen rabbit. Now. Let me find this resort for you.

POCAHONTAS *snatches* JIM*'s phone.*

It's called Magaluf and there's a waterpark and a floating bar. (*Looks at the screen. Freezes.*) Who. The Fuck. Is Ramona?

JIM *looks suddenly terrified.*

JIM. Sorry?

POCAHONTAS (*brandishing his phone*). 'You are now friends with Ramona Eloise Stooke.' Who the fuck is Ramona Eloise Stooke?!

JIM. She's um… She's um –

POCAHONTAS. 'She's-um-she's-um.' Who is she? Tell me who she is? Tell me who she is?

JIM. She's a girl. I met –

POCAHONTAS. Girl? What girl?

JIM. When I was seventeen.

Beat.

POCAHONTAS. Oh my god. Oh my god. Is it her? Is she. *The* girl?

JIM. Yes. She's that girl.

POCAHONTAS. The one that you –

JIM (*quickly*). Yes –

POCAHONTAS. Why are you friends with her on Facebook?

JIM. Just… sent me a friend request.

POCAHONTAS. In her profile picture she's sitting on a rock drinking from a thermos flask. How fucking stupid is that?

JIM. I do that.

POCAHONTAS. Slag.

JIM. You've never met her.

POCAHONTAS. And thank god I never will.

JIM sighs and walks out.

Oi, Jim! Where are you going? (*Beat.*) Thought I was gonna get *plunged*?! (*Beat.*) Jim! I gotta be back at two!

Three

1998.

Beach. Morning. RAMONA (*sixteen, wearing glasses, a cagoule and fleece, and carrying a large rucksack*) *is crouched over a rock pool studying a shell.* JIM (*seventeen*) *enters and watches her for a few moments, unobserved.* RAMONA *prods the shell with her finger.*

JIM. That's a hermit crab.

RAMONA. What?

JIM. That is a hermit crab.

RAMONA. Yes I suspected as much.

JIM. He's actually just borrowed that shell from a deceased gastropod.

RAMONA. Fabulous.

JIM. Most probably a sea snail. So you'd be forgiven if you thought it was a sea snail.

RAMONA. I didn't think it was a sea snail. Actually. Because it has legs. Crucially.

JIM. Correct. Carries his own little mobile home on his back. Wouldn't mind one myself.

RAMONA. How do you know it's a he?

JIM. Females have smooth legs and males have hairy legs. (*Picks it up.*) This one has distinctly hairy legs.

RAMONA (*seductively eyeballing him*). Well, I shave my legs every other day. So yeah, no mistaking I'm one hundred per cent priiiime female...

Beat.

JIM. Cool. Who are you?

RAMONA. I'm –

JIM *holds up a finger to silence her.*

JIM. And why don't you try and answer it in five key facts?

RAMONA. Ramona Eloise Stooke of the St Hilda's School for Girls geography field-trip party, Englandshire, sixteen years of age, Capricorn, hate bananas but like banana-flavoured foods, especially antibiotical medicine.

JIM. Antibiotical is not word.

RAMONA. I know that. Your turn.

JIM. Jim Archibald Macdonald of the shittest village in Scotland, aged seventeen, Gemini, future lecturer in naturalism at the Royal Society, hate raisins *in* things but like them in isolation.

RAMONA. Very good.

JIM. What brings you to my humble homeland, Ramona Eloise Stooke of Englandshire?

RAMONA. An investigation into what human and physical forces are currently driving change in the Scottish Highlands landscape.

JIM. Fascinating.

RAMONA (*defensive*). It is actually.

JIM. I wasn't being sarcastic.

RAMONA. Oh. Good. That's refreshing. Most people are.

JIM. I'm incredibly interested in the erosion of the coastline. See the headland over there?

RAMONA. Yup.

JIM. One day that won't exist. It'll just crumble into the sea bit by bit and one day I'll wake up and… Poof! It'll be gone. Have you been crying?

RAMONA. No.

JIM. You look like you have.

RAMONA. I suffer from an acute allergy to silver birches.

JIM. There are very few silver birches on the West Coast.

RAMONA. I've seen you before you know.

JIM. Have you indeed?

RAMONA. At our caravan site we're staying at.

JIM. I've seen you too.

RAMONA. Are you like the caravan skivvy or something?

JIM. Er, no I'm not a skivvy. 'Skivvyy'?! Honestly! (*Beat.*) No, Darren's the skivvy. He does the shitty jobs like scrubbing the toilets. I'm one up from him. Even though he's two years older than me. Sort of his line manager. Rumour has it he's a massive perv.

RAMONA. Oh dear oh dear. I don't like the sound of pervs, Jim. From what I've heard.

JIM. My dad thinks everyone's just shit-stirring. Helps Darren out because we own the site. But he is definitely a perv. His eyes are very close together.

RAMONA. You can never trust someone with eyes that are very close together, can you?

JIM. No. I like your fleece.

RAMONA. Thank you. It's a two-forty gsm Regatta fleece. Totally windproof and it has an anti-pill lining.

JIM. What's anti-pill?

RAMONA. You know when you wash it and it goes all bobbly?

JIM. Oh I hate that –

RAMONA. Bane of my life –

JIM. Tell me about it –

RAMONA. But not this one. This one stays super-smooth.

JIM. Cool.

RAMONA. Go on. Feel it.

JIM *gets closer to* RAMONA *and rubs the sleeve. Their eyes lock briefly. A sensual moment.*

JIM. Very nice. Very soft. Very anti-pilly.

RAMONA *suddenly breaks away, unable to handle the searing sexual tension.*

RAMONA. Saw a seal this morning. Popped its head out the water and when I waved, it blinked at me as if it was saying hello.

JIM. Sure it wasn't a selkie?

RAMONA. What's that?

JIM. A selkie is a mythological creature harking from the sea. Put simply it is a seal that can shed its skin to become human upon land. Selkies can live a completely normal life as a human and no one will ever know they're actually a selkie because they keep their seal skin hidden away. They might even be married and have another seal wife and a whole family in the sea. Quite cool no?

RAMONA. Fascinating. And I'm not being sarcastic.

JIM. I could be a selkie for all you know or indeed you could be one.

RAMONA. I'm definitely not.

JIM. Well, I could be.

RAMONA. Don't think so. But if I do happen to find a seal skin lying around, I'll reconsider it as a possibility.

JIM. Why were those girls running away from you?

RAMONA. Sorry?

JIM. When I arrived you were with a bunch of girls but they ran away from you.

RAMONA. They didn't run away. They just left.

JIM. Why were they laughing?

RAMONA. Because I'd just told an incredibly witty joke. Plus, I'll be honest, Jim, I love my own company.

JIM. I enjoy my own company too.

RAMONA. Me too.

JIM. If I could hang out with myself all the time it would be ideal.

RAMONA. Oh my god! I think that about myself all the time too! I'm such good company. (*Beat*.) To myself.

JIM. How long are you here for?

RAMONA. Two days.

JIM. Cool.

RAMONA. Cool.

JIM. Cool. Well, if you're knocking around the caravan site later come say hi.

RAMONA. I'll see if I can juggle my diary around.

JIM. Please do. I've got a Chocolate Orange that we could tap and unwrap.

RAMONA. It's not yours. It's Terry's.

JIM. No it is mine. I bought it.

RAMONA. No I know. I meant… Doesn't matter.

JIM. Oh right – yeah I get it. It's Terry's Chocolate Orange. That's funny.

RAMONA. I know, thank you. That's just my sense of humour.

JIM. Sure. (*Pointing.*) My caravan's that one by the large Scots pine. If you bark three times like a seal I'll let you in.

RAMONA. What does a seal sound like exactly?

JIM *barks like a seal.*

JIM. Like that.

RAMONA *mimics.*

RAMONA. Like that?

JIM. Well no. Not exactly. But I'll certainly know if it's you.

RAMONA. Yes you will. (*Coquettish.*) In more ways than one.

JIM. How do you mean?

RAMONA. I dunno really, I was being… coquettish.

JIM. Coquettish? Sure. Cool.

RAMONA. Yeah. Cool.

Awkward beat. JIM *takes a jar out of his bag, picks up the hermit crab, and puts it in the jar.*

What are you going to do with that?

JIM. I'm going to preserve it for ever in this little jar.

RAMONA. How strange. Will you kill him then?

JIM. He'll just go to sleep and never wake up.

RAMONA. So basically yes.

JIM. All in the name of science.

RAMONA. Crab killer!

JIM. Ha. Yeah.

RAMONA. Okay well, maybe see ya later. Jim.

JIM. Yeah. See ya. Ramona.

> RAMONA *skips off.* JIM *watches her go and then stands alone on stage inspecting the hermit crab in the jar. He taps the glass.*

Four

2013.

The next day. JIM *(thirty-two), wearing a cagoule and a pair of binoculars round his neck, addresses the audience. He grows increasingly agitated throughout this speech and is intermittently bitten by midges.*

JIM. The island you can see in the distance, is the Island of Mull and is the second largest island in the Inner Hebrides – famed for its Isle of Mull cheddar cheese. This very robust cheddar is known for its distinctive crumbly consistency and tangy finish on the tongue. The Island of Mull is often confused with Mull of Kintyre – which is the subject of a song by Paul McCartney and his band Wings, which included his late wife Linda, a prominent vegetarian. It is not known if Linda was a fan of Isle of Mull cheddar, but she was certainly *able* to eat it, as she was never a full vegan…

> *Someone leaves.*

Oh sorry the tour isn't actually over, sir… No understood, understood. Bye now. Thank you so much for coming. So kind. Bye bye. (*Beat*.) And um yes… This headland has eroded substantially over the past decade, but once stretched out a staggering fifteen metres further into the Atlantic. On a clear day you can see the Islands of Eigg, Muck and Rum… but today, alas, the thick fog means that we cannot see them. At all.

JIM *slaps his face quite viciously to get rid of a midge. He is now very agitated.*

Right! Yes well… We've reached the end of our tour so thank you, everyone. My name is Jim and this is my tour. I run it independently and if you enjoyed it, please spread the word or leave a review on Trip Advisor. Anything less than four stars and I'll personally hunt you down and gut you like a fish! Haha! (*Beat*.) No. Being silly. Okay. Well. At midday I will be doing my Rock-Pool Ramble… Meeting point is at The Brae Inn… Hope you enjoyed the tour. Lovely… See you at the Rock-Pool Ramble?… That's fine. No, that's absolutely fine. Perfect. Perfect.

JIM *watches his audience retreat and sighs.*

Five

1998.

JIM*'s caravan. Evening.* JIM *has his hand down his trousers. He is not masturbating, but squeezing his genitals absentmindedly.* RAMONA *enters and barks like a seal.*

RAMONA. Ow! Ow! Ow!

JIM. Fuck!

RAMONA *does an elaborate curtsey.*

RAMONA. Good afternoon, Sir Jim of Scotlandshire!

JIM. Do you not knock?

RAMONA. Oh. I was doing the seal bark. As per arranged?

JIM. Yeah I actually thought you'd knock and then do the seal bark?

RAMONA. That wasn't clear in your instructions.

JIM. Well. Anyway. (*Coquettish.*) Hi.

RAMONA (*also coquettish*). Hi. What are you up to, baby? (*Beat.*) I mean babe. Not baby. Babe.

JIM. Chilling, babe.

RAMONA. Cool.

JIM. And thinking.

RAMONA. What were you thinking about?

JIM. I was… thinking about why the hairs on your arms and legs don't grow as long as the hairs on your head?

RAMONA. One of the many mysteries of life, Jim. I've got lots of hair. (*Beat.*) On my head. Not sort of in my pits or on my you know… (*Indicates crotch.*)

JIM (*quickly*). Yes that's fine.

Neither of them know what to say next. RAMONA *arranges herself in a seductive position.*

RAMONA. Have you ever been to the Greek islands, Jimmy? Do you mind if I call you Jimmy, Jimmy?

JIM. No. And no I haven't.

RAMONA. Oh you must, you must! The jewels of the Aegean Sea. According to Thomas Cook. I went to the pine-clad island of Paxos last year, Jimmy. Cats everywhere. They cull them apparently. Conk them over the heads with jars of olives.

JIM. Ouch! Did you um… go with a lover or –

RAMONA. A what?

JIM. A lover?

RAMONA. A lover? Oh no. I haven't got a boyfriend, at this very moment. In time. Lot of options of course. Fingers in proverbial pies. But um no. Currently, I'm a single Pringle ready to mingle! I am, as it were, unattached.

JIM. Me too.

RAMONA. Cool. Me too.

JIM. Yeah. Me too.

RAMONA. Yeah cool. Me too.

JIM. Yeah. Who'd you go with then? To the 'pine-clad island of Paxos'?

RAMONA. My mum.

JIM. That's nice.

RAMONA. No not really. She's having a breakdown because she's a single mother in her late forties with little hope of ever finding love again.

JIM. Plenty of older women find love again. Edwina Currie for example.

RAMONA. My mum won't, she's not a very nice person, plus she's going through the menopause and has developed a subtle but noticeable moustache. Do you like your mum?

JIM. I would if she was here.

RAMONA. Where is she?

JIM. Not sure exactly. I mean she's dead.

RAMONA. Oh.

JIM. But she was cremated and my dad threw her ashes in what he thought was the loch just beyond Ardmore, but it is actually a reservoir. So there's about an eight per cent chance I've drunk her. Which I have mixed feelings about.

RAMONA. Yum! *Not!* Ha!

JIM. Ha. Yeah.

RAMONA. If it's any consolation, I kind of wish my mum was dead.

JIM. You probably don't.

RAMONA. I do.

JIM. Okay.

RAMONA *energetically sniffs* JIM.

RAMONA. Don't tell me. CK One?

JIM. Couple of squirts.

RAMONA. Unisex. Niiiice.

JIM. Yeah. So cool that it's unisex.

RAMONA. Yeah. Love unisex. Because it's like both sexes can wear it?

JIM. Yeah so cool. Both sexes can wear it.

RAMONA. Yeah. Unisex. Niiice.

JIM. Yeah. Unisex. Niiice. Yeah…

Beat.

RAMONA. Do you have any music, Jimmy?

JIM. Does Batman wear a cloak?

RAMONA. What?

JIM. Yes I've got music, babe. What kind of stuff you in to? House? Drum 'n' bass?

RAMONA. Enya Patricia Brennan mainly. More commonly known as, simply, Enya. Her *Watermark* album is outstanding – sends shivers down my spine. I like listening to 'Orinoco Flow' while having a candlelit bath. (*Beat.*) In the nude. (*Beat.*) Obviously. Because I'm in the bath.

A moment. They regard each other.

JIM. I like Enya too. And 'Orinoco Flow' is possibly her most accomplished song to date. And as it happens I have recently obtained her famous *Watermark* album for myself.

JIM wiggles in a silly way.

Would you like to flow to 'Orinoco Flow'?

RAMONA mirrors him.

RAMONA. Yes, I would like to flow to 'Orinoco Flow'. Let me just oil up the limbs.

RAMONA limbers up while JIM puts on the CD.

JIM. May I have this dance, *madame*?

RAMONA. *Oui oui, monsieur.*

Enya comes on. They start dancing very energetically to 'Orinoco Flow'.

God, doesn't get better than this, does it?

JIM. Tell me about it.

RAMONA. Wow! I didn't know my body was even capable of moving like this! It's amazing!

JIM stops dancing and watches RAMONA dance for a few moments.

JIM. You are a genuinely astounding dancer, Ramona.

RAMONA. Thank you, I know. Got quite flexible hips – so I'm told.

JIM. You do. Great swivel.

RAMONA. But my hamstrings are very tight – so my squat is limited.

RAMONA demonstrates her squat.

JIM. What you talking about? That's really low!

RAMONA. Thanks. I think I get on better with boys.

JIM. Yeah?

RAMONA. Yeah. Don't really like the girls at my school. They find me quite amusing apparently and satirise my sexual-innocence via comparisons to nuns and B-list characters from biblical texts.

JIM. Does it bother you?

RAMONA. No, not really. I mean, obviously it can be very lonely and I yearn for the acceptance of my peers but, apart from that, it really doesn't affect me. At all. Hahaha!

Beat. They stop dancing. They look at each other.

Sometimes I feel like your eyes are burning into my soul.

JIM. I'm just looking at you.

RAMONA. Yeah I know. That's what I meant.

JIM *lunges at* RAMONA.

Wait!

RAMONA *removes her glasses, takes two Trebor Extra Strong Mints from her pocket and pops one into* JIM*'s mouth and one into hers. They crunch them quickly whilst staring intensely at each other.*

Okay. I'm ready.

They launch at each other with gusto and kiss vigorously for some time. They stop – wipe saliva from their faces.

JIM. There's going to be a meteor shower tomorrow night, Ramona. It's a Leonid meteor shower. They occur when the earth passes through the debris left by the comet Tempel–Tuttle. It only happens every fifteen years. Do you wanna see it with me?

RAMONA. What? In fifteen years?

JIM. No, tomorrow. But in fifteen years as well if you fancy.

RAMONA. Cool. Yeah okay. How do we watch it?

JIM (*mysterious*). Meet me under the Scots pine at exactly twenty-hundred hours aka nightfall and I'll take you down to the beach...

Six

2013.

The beach. The next day. Morning. JIM is inspecting something in a bucket. POCAHONTAS runs on in a panic.

POCAHONTAS. Jim! Oh my god, Jim, there you are! Why are you not picking up? I've called you seventeen times and you haven't replied to a single one of my twenty-six texts!

JIM. Signal can be a bit patchy here.

POCAHONTAS. You've got absolutely brilliant signal and you've been standing here for over a quarter of an hour. (*Peers in bucket.*) What the fuck is that? Looks like a bucket of sick.

JIM. How d'you know I've been standing here? That's a jellyfish. Have you been watching me?

POCAHONTAS. I've been monitoring your movements all morning. Have you heard of the app 'Find Your Friends'? It's absolutely fantastic. I installed it on your phone yesterday so I can keep track of your whereabouts at all times.

JIM. Well, that is obviously absolutely terrifying.

POCAHONTAS. I was getting worried. I thought you might have committed suicide because of your depressed state.

JIM. Take it off my phone now.

POCAHONTAS. I'm afraid that's not possible, Jim, because circumstances have changed. I am now linked to you for ever by the strongest possible bond and will need constant and instant responses twenty-four hours a day, seven days a week.

JIM. Can you tell me what you're talking about?

POCAHONTAS. I am with child. I am prrrregnant.

Beat.

JIM. Okay. Is this one of your –

POCAHONTAS. No.

JIM. But you're on the pill.

POCAHONTAS. *Was* on the pill. Basically my friend Kelly-Anne posted something on Facebook about how the hormones are quite shit or… well, I can't remember the details – so I made the executive decision to –

JIM. Who the fuck is Kelly-Anne?

POCAHONTAS. I don't know her personally. She's got a tarantula.

JIM. Jesus! I mean… Are you sure?

POCAHONTAS. Four tests, Jim. Four little windows saying pregnant pregnant pregnant, pregnant, so yeah I'm sure I'm pregnant.

JIM. Fuck. Okay. Is it… (*Beat.*) Is it mine then?

POCAHONTAS. Is it mine? Did you just say that?

JIM. I did yes.

POCAHONTAS. Is it mine?

JIM. Yes – is it mine?

POCAHONTAS. I can't believe you're asking me that. I'm fucking shocked.

JIM. Okay. But is it mine though?

POCAHONTAS. Is it mine?! You've just asked it again!

JIM. Yes is it mine because you haven't answered – is it mine?

POCAHONTAS. Is it mine?!

JIM. Yes! Is it mine?

POCAHONTAS. Of course it's yours, you fat fucking prick.

JIM. Okay. Jesus. Okay. Fuck. It's mine. It's mine.

Beat.

POCAHONTAS. Probably. (*Off* JIM*'s look.*) I mean obviously I can't be a hundred per cent.

JIM. What do you mean you can't be a hundred per cent?

POCAHONTAS. Men are drawn to me. Moths and flames, Jimmy. Moths and flames…

JIM. We'll get a proper test done.

POCAHONTAS. Honestly, you don't know how lucky you are to have me as the future mother of your child. I'm nineteen, I'm fucking fit, I've got a pierced clitoris and I'm double-jointed. You can basically bend me up like a pretzel and take me up the yin-yang. What's not to love? You're an ex-con who works in a fish factory –

JIM. Fish merchants' –

POCAHONTAS. And you're *thirty-two*. You're basically dead.

JIM. Be quiet! Be quiet for just a fucking second please! (*Gathering himself.*) Pocahontas, we're going to the clinic. As soon as I get back from Frankfurt we are going to the clinic and then afterwards, we're going to sit down and talk to each other. And not just talk, most importantly, listen. You need to actually listen for once.

POCAHONTAS. It's amazing, Jim, isn't it? Just to think: there's a little piece of you. Growing inside of me. Like one of your crusty wee sea monsters –

JIM. Crustacea.

POCAHONTAS. Except rather than being a dead thing from the past trapped inside a jar, this one will actually slither out and live. I hope she's a girl, Jim. I'd love to have a wee girl. Dress her up in satin party dresses and buy her jam tarts and brush her hair. What you think of the name Jasmina? Or Rapunzel! I'm never, ever going to cut her hair, it's just going to trail along behind her like a long, golden waterfall. Can you imagine?

JIM puts his head in his hands.

JIM. Please, Pocahontas. Please be quiet.

A couple of beats of silence.

POCAHONTAS. Don't be sad, Jim. Why are you always so sad when everything is so amazing?

Seven

1998.

Beach. The next day. Evening. It is dark. The moon is bright. The sound of the sea. RAMONA *(sixteen) and* JIM *(seventeen) are facing each other.*

RAMONA. Hello, boy.

JIM. Hello, girl.

They turn to face the audience, hold hands and look up at the sky. A moment or two.

RAMONA *(singing slightly self-consciously).* Starry starry night!

She trails off.

JIM. You look sad.

RAMONA. Those pesky silver birches wreaking havoc on my tear ducts as per. Also Josephine Woodcock put a soiled sanitary towel in my sleeping bag. Which I didn't love. Have you had a nice day?

JIM. Average slash just below average. I watched three back-to-back episodes of *Buffy the Vampire Slayer*, learnt the anatomy of a sea urchin archaically known as a sea hedgehog off by heart, then I had to remove the limescale from shower cubicle six, which should be Darren's job but someone asked him to DJ for your party and my dad let him... What was his music like then? Bet it was shit.

RAMONA. Dunno really. Just normal. Didn't play 'Orinoco Flow'.

JIM. Scandalous.

Beat. They both stare up at the sky.

Any second now. Any second now we will witness the enchanting trail of debris left by the comet Tempel–Tuttle...

A few beats. They watch.

Not always bang on time.

RAMONA. I'm not in any rush.

JIM. Seen any more seals?

RAMONA. No.

JIM. Seen any more selkies?

RAMONA. Not that I know of.

JIM. Legend has it that selkies typically seek those who are dissatisfied with their life. Do you think that could be you, Ramona?

RAMONA. No. I'm a very, very, incredibly happy person.

JIM. Are you?

RAMONA. Dunno actually. Never really thought about it before. Are you a very, very, incredibly happy person?

JIM. No. I often feel deeply troubled.

RAMONA. Cool. (*Beat*.) I mean not cool. But, cool, I understand.

Slight pause. RAMONA *is looking at the floor*.

JIM. Are you crying?

RAMONA. A little bit…

JIM. Why?

RAMONA. I feel sad for you, Jim. And I feel sad for your dead mum and I feel sad for my alive mum, because I think she's a slut and she's very unhappy. She bought and returned nine dogs this year and I'll never see them again and I liked them so much – I mean *nine* dogs?! And I feel sad for myself because I had the decency to go into Josephine Woodcock's tent when she was sleeping and very kindly cleaned out her hairbrush and she didn't appreciate it and they all hate me those girls at my school and my mum hates me…

JIM. Did you know that if a girl wishes to make contact with a selkie male, she must shed seven tears into the sea?

RAMONA *doesn't respond*.

I don't hate you.

RAMONA. I don't hate you either.

JIM *suddenly looks up at the sky. There are flashing lights*.

JIM. Oh look, Ramona! It's happening!

RAMONA. Whoa!

The meteor shower illuminates the stage and RAMONA *and* JIM *gaze up at it for a few moments in silence.*

I think this is the most beautiful spectacle I've ever seen in my life.

JIM. It makes you feel like nothing matters. We're just specks of dust.

RAMONA. Yeah like if we died right now – I wouldn't care.

JIM. I wouldn't want to die right now.

RAMONA. No I actually wouldn't either.

They stand watching this spectacle for a few moments. The meteor shower dies down.

(*Staring intensely at* JIM.) I feel intensely alive.

JIM (*staring intensely at* RAMONA). I feel like my soul has entered another dimension.

RAMONA (*staring intensely at* JIM). I feel like every nerve in my body is tingly, like I'm on fire but in a good way not a painful way.

JIM. I feel like… Like I've been turned inside out and the world is upside down and everything is back to front but it all just makes *perfect* sense. Do you know what I mean?

RAMONA. Absolutely.

JIM. Ramona?

RAMONA. Jim?

JIM. You know last night?

RAMONA. Yes.

JIM. When you burst into my caravan without knocking?

RAMONA. Yes. But if you recall, Jimmy, we did prearrange the seal bark?

JIM. Right whatever. And I told you that I was thinking about the hairs on my arms?

RAMONA. Yes.

JIM. I wasn't doing that.

RAMONA. Oh.

JIM. I was actually about to have a wank.

RAMONA. Don't know what to say to that.

JIM. Do you know who I was going to think about?

RAMONA. Shania Twain?

JIM. No.

RAMONA. Zoë Ball?

JIM. No.

RAMONA. Wh– who were you gonna think about then?

JIM. I was going to think about you.

RAMONA. Ha! Er, wow.

JIM. Is that disgusting?

RAMONA. No I mean yes but. No. I don't think anyone's ever thought about me while wanking before.

JIM. Well, they have now.

RAMONA (*Ferrero Rocher advert*). Exchellente!

JIM. Do you want to make love, Ramona?

RAMONA. Quite possibly maybe I'd like to do that.

JIM. Is that a yes then?

RAMONA. Yes. I mean I haven't actually been you know… Deflowered yet but happy to pull the plug.

JIM. Good news. Well. Allow me to… do the honours.

RAMONA. Will do, will do.

JIM. I too of course am a… novice in the departmento sexualiano.

RAMONA. What?

JIM. I'm a… virgin.

RAMONA. Wicked!

JIM. And um just before we... commence. I'd like to read to you – my self-penned haiku.

RAMONA. What's a haiku?

JIM. A short Japanese poem. That I've written about... Well, you.

RAMONA looks embarrassed and pleased.

RAMONA. Oh wow. Thank you. I'm flattered, Jim.

JIM removes a scrap of paper from his pocket.

JIM. You, you coal-haired maiden from the south
Did find ye hermit crab on yon beach
But you also found a moist Scottish mouth.

RAMONA. Wow, that's amazing, Jim. You're a wonderful poet.

JIM. Thank you, I know.

Beat.

RAMONA. Well... Time for these motherfuckers to lose their V-plates!

Beat. Neither of them moves.

So... Shoes first or?

JIM. Um... Tops probably.

RAMONA. Tops? Cool. Fab. I'll just... (*Tries to remove her fleece.*) Dammit! My fleece is stuck – the zip's jammed.

[*N.B. Their speech can overlap during the following exchange.*]

JIM. Pull it over your head?

RAMONA (*panicked*). It won't go over my head! The neck hole's too small!

JIM. That's okay. Leave it on.

RAMONA. Cool. Still got my wellies on, is that a problem?

JIM. They can stay on.

RAMONA. They're very easy to remove?

JIM. I honestly don't care.

JIM *goes to kiss her.* RAMONA *pulls back.*

RAMONA. Okay. And do you have such a thing as a um... sheath?

JIM. A what?

RAMONA. A condominium?

JIM. Oh right yes. Of course.

JIM *fumbles around in his pocket and produces a condom.*

RAMONA (*bothered*). Oh got it right there! Handy!

JIM. Ha – well yeah. Been in there for ages.

RAMONA. Ha! Gathering dust! (*Beat.*) Cool. Right. (*Coquettish.*) Allow me to remove your cargo shorts, Jim.

JIM. Leave them!

RAMONA. No – please, my pleasure.

JIM. Seriously leave them. They're quite tight and you have to kind of really wiggle to... So I'll just go through the files.

JIM *unzips his flies.*

RAMONA. Coolio. Well, I'll just hitch this up and um... take my... drawers down so that you can –

JIM. Yup.

JIM *tears open the condom and self-consciously puts it on.*

Luverley.

RAMONA. Right. Is the um... beast robed?

JIM. Sure is.

RAMONA. All aboard! Honk honk!

JIM. Ha yeah. Watch out, it could get choppy!

RAMONA (*like a pirate*). Oooh arrr!

JIM. Okay. Ready?

RAMONA. Yup.

JIM. Tell me if it hurts.

RAMONA. It won't.

JIM *tentatively thrusts*. RAMONA *winces*.

Okay yeah that does hurt a bit.

JIM *stops*.

JIM. Sorry.

RAMONA. No but in a good way… Like please continue.

JIM. Are you sure?

RAMONA. Definitely.

JIM *begins to thrust gently for a few beats*.

JIM. Is this fast enough?

RAMONA. Yup.

JIM. Cos I can go faster?

RAMONA. No that's a perfect… tempo. Like iambic pentameter.

JIM. Ha. Cool. Are you enjoying it?

RAMONA. Yes! Yes I am! Enjoying it like hell!

JIM. Good! Me too!

JIM *climaxes. A short pause*.

RAMONA. Is that – ?

JIM. It's over yes.

Long pause. They sit back up again.

Normally last longer than that.

RAMONA (*quickly*). I don't mind.

Pause.

I love you… Jim.

JIM. Thank you. I love you… Ramona.

RAMONA. Thank you.

JIM. That was amazing.

RAMONA. Yeah.

JIM. We should do that again.

RAMONA. Yeah. Not now, but –

JIM. No. At some point. When are you leaving?

RAMONA. Tomorrow. With the noonday sun.

JIM. That's soon.

RAMONA. Yeah.

> RAMONA *zips up her fleece.*

> (*Yorkshire accent for this line.*) Lovely. Well, I'll just…
> (*As she pulls up pants.*) Oop they go.

JIM. Yep. I'll put me tee back on.

RAMONA. There we are… Good as new!

JIM. Yep.

RAMONA (*Scottish accent for this line*). Aye.

> *Pause.*

> It's funny that's just it, isn't it?

JIM. How do you mean?

RAMONA. That's that. That's sex. Done and dusted.

JIM. Cool. Yeah. You liked it though, didn't you?

RAMONA. Oh yes. (*Like a cowgirl.*) Oh yeehah! It was lush!

> *Beat.*

JIM. Are you going to go back to that bonfire-sausage-bonanza
party now then?

RAMONA. I suppose I ought to show my face.

JIM. Go and listen to Darren's crap DJing. Pig in shit. He'll be
leering all over the girls.

RAMONA. Yeah. (*Beat.*) What? Like perving on them?

JIM. Yeah. I've seen them – I bet he can't believe his luck.

RAMONA. Why do you think he can't believe his luck?

JIM. No. Nothing, I dunno.

> *Slight pause.*

RAMONA. Was that alright?

JIM. Was what alright?

RAMONA. The um, love-making?

JIM. Yeah.

RAMONA. Okay. Great.

JIM. Well, *was* it alright?

RAMONA. You just said it was so, I guess so. I wouldn't know. Felt fine.

JIM. Right. 'Fine.'

RAMONA. Do you mean, leering on all those other girls… Because you've seen them and you think they're –

JIM. He'll leer on them yeah. Cos he's a creep. Why? (*Teasing.*) You getting jealous, Ramona?

RAMONA. Ha! Not likely!

A slight pause.

He's been leering at me too actually. So bloody gross.

JIM. Has he?

RAMONA. Yeah, big time. Undressing me with his eyes. (*Beat.*) And his hands.

JIM. His hands?

RAMONA. Nah, only kidding. But pretty much yeah.

JIM. What do you mean, his hands?

RAMONA. Got a bit handsy, you know. With his hands.

JIM. Handsy. How do you mean, handsy?

RAMONA. Big pervy tentacles all over me –

JIM. Did he touch you?

RAMONA. Sort of. Yeah.

JIM. Touched you how?

RAMONA. Just you know –

JIM. What?

RAMONA. Just like, you know... Stuck his big... hand on me.

JIM. Where?

RAMONA. Um – Well –

JIM. Where, Ramona?

RAMONA. Well... You know?

JIM. No I don't know. Where?

RAMONA. You know in my – in my –

JIM. In your...

RAMONA. Yeah. Yup.

JIM. Fuck.

> JIM *is seething and still.* RAMONA *is worried.*

RAMONA. Whatever. It's not a big deal, it's nothing.

JIM. It's not nothing.

RAMONA. Yeah. I mean I'm obviously a bit traumatised.

JIM. Fuck.

RAMONA. You know I don't think I am that traumatised
actually.

JIM. Did he really do that to you? Did he really touch you?

> RAMONA *hesitates for the tiniest fraction of a second.*

RAMONA. Yes.

Eight

2013.

The beach. Lunchtime. JIM *addresses the audience in his cagoule.*

JIM. These rock pools are full of common mussels, indeed these are the same mussels you'd find in your moules marinière. Although here of course, they are not swimming in cream and white-wine sauce, but salt water! (*Beat.*) Mussels can't actually swim of course, in fact they barely move. Normally spending their entire lifespan clamped onto the same area of rock. Ha! Know the bloody feeling! Hahaha! (*Beat.*) Right well... We've reached the end of our tour so thank you, everyone. My name is Jim and this is my tour. I run it independently and if you enjoyed it, spread the word or leave a review on Trip Advisor. Anything less than four stars and I'll hunt you down and gut you like a fish! Haha! But in all seriousness – please replace your specimens carefully back in their natural habitat and I request you *not* to take away your buckets. They are *not* free. I repeat, they are *not* free. They are one pound and seventy-five pence each... So. Just please don't take them away. Because they are *not* free. Right! Bye bye now. Thank you. Bye bye...

JIM *watches his audience retreat and sighs.* RAMONA *enters from the audience.* JIM *looks at her for a few beats in shock.*

Fuck.

RAMONA. I know.

JIM. Fuck.

RAMONA. I know. Yeah.

JIM. Fuck. (*Beat.*) Sorry.

RAMONA. I know.

A slight pause.

Hello, Jimmy.

JIM. Hello, Ramona.

Another slight pause.

RAMONA. It's good to see you.

JIM. Yes. Good to see you too.

RAMONA. You look so –

JIM. What?

RAMONA. Different.

JIM. Different? Different in what way?

RAMONA. Not different in a bad way.

JIM. Is it my hair? It's my hair, isn't it? Sometimes I get puffy
hair.

RAMONA. No no – your hair's great.

JIM. Cool. Your hair's great too. You look sort of the same
actually.

RAMONA. That's disappointing.

JIM. Is it?

RAMONA. Yeah.

JIM. I'm not sure it is.

   A slight pause. RAMONA *eyes* JIM's *bucket.*

RAMONA. What have you got there?

JIM. Lion's mane jellyfish?

RAMONA. 'Lion's mane'. Cool.

JIM. Their stinging tentacles can be as long as a hundred feet.

RAMONA. Ouch! That would be a painful sting!

JIM. It's highly unlikely you would get stung as they tend to
drift in very, very deep water.

RAMONA. Right.

JIM. They sometimes wash up after a storm. (*Intense.*) But yes.
If you did happen to be in very, very deep water and you did
get stung then it would be incredibly painful. In fact it would
probably paralyse you.

RAMONA. Wow. Okay.

JIM. Sorry. I'm being very serious, I don't know why I'm being so serious. Sorry. To be honest I have absolutely no idea what to say to you.

RAMONA. That's fine. That's normal.

JIM. Nice suit.

RAMONA. Thank you. It's the only thing I've got with me. I came straight from work. Last night. Actually.

JIM. Up from London?

RAMONA (*rambling*). Yeah, just hopped on a train, after some work drinks, I'd had a few drinks, I was a bit drunk if I'm being honest, it was someone's birthday and I'd had a long day so I was tired and yeah very drunk cos I'd had a few drinks at this drinks thing and just decided to hop on an overnight train very drunk. (*Beat.*) It's a bit weird, isn't it?

JIM. No. Not at all.

RAMONA. It is. Me coming here. It is a bit weird. I know it is.

JIM. Well. Yes. It is. I suppose. But I'm very glad that you did.

RAMONA. Good. It's the Leonid meteor shower tonight, isn't it?

Beat.

JIM. It was last night.

RAMONA. Oh.

JIM. You missed it.

RAMONA. Oh. I thought… Did you see it?

JIM. It was cloudy.

RAMONA. Shame.

JIM. Yes.

RAMONA. But you were looking for it?

JIM. What?

RAMONA. You went to look for it?

JIM. I was out and about.

RAMONA. Okay…

JIM. Quite a surprise.

RAMONA. Well yes.

JIM. Seeing you.

RAMONA. Yes.

JIM. After all this time.

RAMONA. Fifteen years.

JIM. And one day.

A slight pause.

That's why you travelled six hundred miles, is it? To see the meteor shower?

RAMONA. Yes. Pretty much. But also… I wanted to tell you something.

Beat.

JIM. Tell me what?

RAMONA (*suddenly*). Not here.

JIM. Um. Okay. Where?

RAMONA. Dunno. Just not on. A beach. Or now.

JIM. Sure.

RAMONA. I'm sorry. This is crazy. I'm just a crazy woman who's turned up in Scotland. On a beach. In a suit. On the wrong day. And it's just a very, very unhinged thing to do. I'm sorry. I don't really know what I'm doing. Sorry.

JIM. Stop apologising.

RAMONA. Sorry. Okay. Sorry I'll stop saying sorry! Haha. I feel like I wanted this to be better. The first meeting. I wanted it to be better.

JIM. It's fine. It's honestly absolutely fine. It's fantastic actually. I mean… Can you give me a couple of hours? I just have to… What are you doing tonight? Have you got plans tonight? Where are you staying?

RAMONA. I don't know. Amazingly. I don't really know what I'm doing.

JIM. Because… I've got quite a large lasagne in the freezer.

RAMONA. Right.

JIM. Probably stupid but I could… defrost it and open up a bottle of Blossom Hill?

RAMONA. Sure. Okay. I mean, literally what else can I do?

JIM. And… also you'd like to?

RAMONA. Oh yeah, that too. No, genuinely. (*Beat.*) Do you actually want to see me? You're not just being polite, are you? Because I've travelled for nine hours and look like a scarecrow?

JIM. Yes I do want to see you. And you don't look like a scarecrow… So… shall I give you my number then?

Nine

2013. JIM's flat. That afternoon. JIM, *enters clutching a bottle of Blossom Hill.* POCAHONTAS, *dressed up and giddy with excitement, bounds up to greet him. He looks alarmed.*

POCAHONTAS. Hello, darling! Did you have a lovely day? (*Eyeing wine.*) Ooh Blossom Hill. Let me take your fleece for you – you must be exhausted!

JIM. What are you doing here?

POCAHONTAS *removes his fleece and kisses him passionately.* JIM *eventually manages to extract himself.*

How… How the hell did you get in?

POCAHONTAS *jangles a set of keys.*

POCAHONTAS. Took the liberty of getting myself a wee set of keys cut. Do you mind? I didn't think you'd mind. (*Off* JIM's *look.*) Oh no, you do mind, don't you?

JIM. Yes, I do mind. I do mind very much. You can't just… Fuck. You can't just get keys cut, that's… Jesus Christ!

POCAHONTAS. Oh don't be angry, Jim! When you're out I can pop in and water your spider plants, put the dinner on, that kind of thing. I bought you a sixteen-ounce rib-eye steak and an air freshener and everything!

POCAHONTAS *suddenly produces a can of Glade air freshener and starts to spray it around the room.*

Just trying to get rid of that heinous whiff! Do you think it could be a rotting rat under the floorboards? I cannot abide the odour of decaying rodents –

JIM. It's not a rat. I do not have rats. Look… I'm afraid…You're probably going to have to –

POCAHONTAS. Leave? I'm one hundred per cent not leaving. So I would dispel that thought from your mind right now. Because your lottery numbers have come up, my friend – I'm making you steak avec pommes frites and giving you the best blowjob of your sorry little life.

JIM. Pokie, I've got to pack. I've got to prepare for Frankfurt. You know – lots of things to do. Packing. Online check-in. You know. Tons of things. Packing. You know. And the online check-in, as I say. Tons of things.

POCAHONTAS *sits herself down.*

POCAHONTAS. Have you ever been inside a new-build, Jim? One of those new-build houses in a cul-de-sac? Wimpey homes. Like a giant doll's house. Absolutely *stunning*. Completely white inside with cream carpets so thick you feel like you're walking on clouds. Well. Listen to this. I've just had a viewing of a show home aaaand plot 16A will be available in two months and it has a corner jacuzzi bath, under-floor heating and lattice-effect, triple-glazed windows! What do you think, Jim – shall we make an offer? Shall we go to Land of Leather and get a three-piece suede suite with a matching armchair recliner?

JIM. You know what? That all sounds delightful, Pokie. You're right, I'm a big fan of new-builds. And hearing you talk about it just then was very interesting and exciting. So. Let's talk it about, shall we? But. Let's talk about it when I get back from Frankfurt. Okay? I promise.

POCAHONTAS (*surprised*). Really?

JIM. Yes. We'll talk about it.

POCAHONTAS. Wow. Cool. Okay. You really want to talk about it?

JIM. I do yes. I do want to talk about it.

POCAHONTAS. I feel so fucking happy right now.

JIM. Yes.

POCAHONTAS. So happy I could just stay…

POCAHONTAS *pauses on the threshold of the door and looks straight into* JIM*'s eyes.*

I think we're soulmates, Jim. (*Beat.*) Don't you?

JIM (*quiet*). Yeah.

POCAHONTAS. I love you.

POCAHONTAS *looks at him expectantly.*

JIM. And I also… love… you.

JIM *tries to close the door.* POCAHONTAS *wedges her foot in the door.*

POCAHONTAS. How much?

JIM. A lot.

POCAHONTAS. How much is a lot?

JIM. Like a lot a lot.

POCAHONTAS. Quantify it.

JIM. I love you so much that I could… just…

POCAHONTAS. Just what?

JIM. Just… Um. Just probably… marry you?

Beat.

POCAHONTAS. Are you fucking kidding me?

JIM. No.

POCAHONTAS. Fuck. That's not what I thought you were going to say at all. Thought it was about going to Spain to eat prawns. Do you really mean that?

JIM looks stricken.

JIM.... Yes. I... want to marry you. But right now –

POCAHONTAS. Oh my god. I can't believe it. I can't believe my actual ears.

JIM. Well. Believe them because it's true.

POCAHONTAS. But just. Wow.

JIM's anger is beginning to rise.

JIM. But right now, my love – you need to leave, sadly. And we will talk about all of this when I get back.

POCAHONTAS. Absolutely. I'm going. I'm going. One quick thing. Three or four tiers? I think four, is better – more classy – but three's my lucky number, so –

JIM. I don't know what you're –

POCAHONTAS. For the cake, Jim, for the cake!

JIM is struggling.

JIM. Now come on, Pocahontas, be a good girl for me.

POCAHONTAS. Okay. But just so you know, I am deeply, deeply religious – I am a woman steeped in the glory of God – so I will be requiring a church wedding-slash-castle if it's nicer, and that is non-fucking-negotiable.

JIM is struggling to keep a lid on his anger.

JIM. Please just... in the nicest possible way. My love. Please just leave.

POCAHONTAS looks defeated.

I'm sorry.

POCAHONTAS (*eyeballing him*). That's okay, Jim. I'm a very understanding and accommodating woman. I'll leave now,

and when you get back from Frankfurt I'm going to be the
best fiancée you've ever met.

POCAHONTAS *exits. JIM stands still for a couple of beats.
Then he suddenly clenches his fists and makes a strange,
strangled whine.*

Ten

2013.

JIM's *flat. Evening. The remnants of a lasagne and a couple of
bottles of wine.* JIM *has gelled his hair back, has funky music
playing and is buoyant.* RAMONA *is sitting on the sofa drinking
a large glass of wine quite rapidly. She is tense. A couple of beats
of silence.*

RAMONA. Hmmm… Lovely.

JIM. Mmm.

Silence. RAMONA *drains her glass of wine.*

RAMONA. Never had a fish lasagne before. Very… tasty.

JIM. Thank you yeah. I work at a fish merchants' specialising in
peat-smoked salmon, kippers, et cetera so I get… free off-cuts.
Of fish.

RAMONA. Lovely. Could I have another glass of wine please?
I'd quite like another glass of wine please if that's okay with
you, to have another glass of wine?

JIM. Sure.

JIM *pours her another wine. She takes a couple of large glugs.*

RAMONA. Lovely wine!

RAMONA *suddenly stands up and surveys* JIM's *specimens
in formaldehyde. She picks one up and peers at it.*

Ooh. Who's this little fella?

JIM. Saltwater clam. A skaelop or scallop to those unfamiliar with marine terminology.

RAMONA. Nice! I love scallops.

JIM. Found it while on my biannual beach-combing holiday on Eigg. The island. I'm actually a delegate at this year's international crustacean congress in Frankfurt. Paying to go of course – but still. Flying from Edinburgh Airport tomorrow. Have you ever been to Frankfurt?

RAMONA. No, no I haven't. What does one do at a crustacean congress then?

RAMONA sits down again. Pours herself another glass of wine. Bit fidgety.

JIM. One takes part in an absolutely fantastic meeting, where crustacean biologists from at least sixteen countries come together and discuss their crustacean-based research. Heard of Larry Turbine?

RAMONA. Larry Turbine? No I don't think so.

JIM. He's basically a massively respected taxonomist. From California. Fascinating man... He's um... a bit of a hero of mine actually. And I've sort of been harassing him – well, not harassing him but... Sorry I'm being incredibly boring, aren't I? I think I might have become incredibly boring. I'm sorry.

RAMONA suddenly stands up again.

RAMONA. No, I'm sorry.

JIM. What?

RAMONA. I'm sorry.

Beat. JIM stares at RAMONA.

Because I lied.

A slight pause.

JIM. What about?

RAMONA. I lied.

JIM. Yes?

RAMONA. I lied that I was groped. I lied that, that boy groped me.

JIM. I... I don't understand.

RAMONA. I lied to you, about that boy. Darren – groping me at the caravan site. After we first met. And then I just went back to school and my life and everything went back to normal and you... You went to prison for... Well, I don't know how long –

JIM. Two years. And it was youth detention.

RAMONA. Fuck. And I... I sent you what, like, seven postcards?

JIM. Five.

RAMONA. And then I just sort of... forgot. (*Beat.*) Well, I didn't forget. Obviously I didn't forget. But I wanted to and, for a bit, I almost did. In fact. But then recently, I think about it every day now. That I did that.

Pause.

JIM. He didn't touch you.

RAMONA. No.

JIM. He didn't even touch you.

RAMONA. No.

JIM. Then why did you say he did?

RAMONA. Honestly? I have no idea. It just kind of... popped out.

JIM. Popped out?

RAMONA. Yes.

JIM. What did he do then? What did he actually do to you?

RAMONA. Nothing.

JIM. Nothing?

RAMONA. Nothing.

JIM. Nothing? He did nothing to you?

RAMONA. No.

JIM. So what happened then? What *did* he do to you?

RAMONA. Nothing.

Beat.

JIM. Is this a joke?

RAMONA. No.

JIM. So I… He did nothing.

RAMONA. Yes.

JIM. Why are you telling me this? Now?

RAMONA. Because… Well. I thought you'd probably want to know.

JIM. Okay.

RAMONA. I want to make it better.

JIM. Better for who?

RAMONA. For you.

POCAHONTAS (*offstage*). Bonjour mi amore!

The sound of the door opening. POCAHONTAS *is entering the house.* JIM *jumps up.*

JIM. Fuck.

RAMONA. Who's that?

POCAHONTAS (*offstage*). 'Tis moi! Your tender-footed lover: Pocahontas Shelly Munro.

JIM. Oh god. It's sort of my… Could you just wait in there for a sec? Please?

RAMONA *exits bemused.* POCAHONTAS *barrels into the room with a new Bugaboo pram, in which a Nespresso machine is resting.*

POCAHONTAS. Sorry, I know you're packing, my darling, I'll be out of your hair in a jiffy. But have you ever heard of Eileen Donan Castle, Jim? It's insane! It's basically a huge fairytale castle on the edge of a majestic loch and you can hire the entire place –

JIM. Pokie, I need to explain something to you. (*Eyeing the pram in alarm.*) What is that?

POCAHONTAS. It's a Bugaboo Bee Modern Pastel Pushchair for our soon-to-be-delivered child, and a Nespresso machine for our soon-to-be-delivered John Lewis earthenware coffee cups.

JIM. Look. There's someone else here. The woman from the um… Facebook profile.

POCAHONTAS *freezes*.

POCAHONTAS. The woman from Facebook? *Here?*

JIM. From before. Who got in touch.

POCAHONTAS. She's *here?*

JIM. Yes.

POCAHONTAS. What. The living. Fuck.

RAMONA *enters*.

RAMONA. Hello.

POCAHONTAS *stands stock-still*. RAMONA *looks at* JIM *and back to* POCAHONTAS.

POCAHONTAS. Oh. My. Fucking. God.

JIM. Sssh, calm down.

POCAHONTAS. Oh. My. Fucking. God.

JIM. Please don't do this.

POCAHONTAS. You went to prison for *that?*

JIM. Youth detention and Ramona was here at that time, yes.

POCAHONTAS. Blinded that poor prick for *that?*

Beat.

RAMONA (*shocked*). Blinded him?

JIM (*panicked*). Just in the one eye!

RAMONA. You actually blinded him?

POCAHONTAS. With a pool cue!

JIM. Just in the one eye!

RAMONA. Oh my god I didn't know you blinded him.

POCAHONTAS. His eye fell out.

JIM. No it didn't.

POCAHONTAS. Blood was pouring out of his eyeball.

RAMONA. Fuck.

JIM. You weren't even there! Please stop it. Both of you.

Silence. RAMONA *looks at the floor.* POCAHONTAS *looks her up and down, taking in her trouser suit.*

POCAHONTAS. Is that a trouser suit?

RAMONA. Yes.

POCAHONTAS. Where did you get it?

RAMONA. Zara.

POCAHONTAS. I want a trouser suit. Can I have it?

RAMONA. No.

POCAHONTAS. Why not?

RAMONA. Because it's mine? Sorry, who are you?

POCAHONTAS. Pocahontas.

RAMONA. Pocahontas? That's your actual real name?

POCAHONTAS. Yes that's my actual real name. (*To* JIM.) Why does she talk in that stupid way?

RAMONA (*to* JIM). Is she your... girlfriend?

JIM. Well, we've never put a label on it.

Deathly silence. POCAHONTAS *turns and stares at* JIM.

POCAHONTAS. You just told me you wanted to fucking marry me, you absolute fucking fucker! I am your fucking fiancée! Don't want to put a label on it? (*Pointing at stomach.*) Well, you're gonna have to put a fucking label on this shitty bastard! (*To* RAMONA.) He's got me up the duff, you know?

Beat. RAMONA *takes this in.*

RAMONA. Wow! You're having a baby? That's so cool! Wow!

JIM. Well, we definitely don't know that yet.

POCAHONTAS. Four tests.

RAMONA. Wow! Congratulations! Wow!

POCAHONTAS. Stop saying wow.

JIM. We don't know it's mine yet. Or if indeed there is one at all.

POCAHONTAS. We do.

JIM. We categorically don't.

POCAHONTAS. Been fucking in his Fiat Cinquecento for six months.

JIM. Pocahontas, please. You make it sound so –

POCAHONTAS. So what? Sordid? It is sordid, Jim! It's a peppermint Cinquecento!

JIM. What's wrong with a Cinquecento?!

RAMONA. I like Cinquecentos…

POCAHONTAS *eyes* RAMONA.

POCAHONTAS. Do you like him then? Do you want him to bang the crap out of you?

RAMONA. No.

POCAHONTAS. Do you want him to pummel you into orbit?

RAMONA. No.

POCAHONTAS. Good. Because you can't fucking have him.

RAMONA. That's fine.

POCAHONTAS. You can't fucking have him, love.

RAMONA. Yes, you said.

POCAHONTAS. You. Can. Not. Fucking. Have. Him.

JIM *has his head in his hands.*

JIM. Oh god…

POCAHONTAS. What now?

JIM. I can't... I can't –

POCAHONTAS. Speak up please?

JIM. I just can't –

POCAHONTAS. Can't what? Finish your sentence.

JIM. I can't... This is so fucked. This is so awful. I'm... suffocating.

POCAHONTAS. I think you're being melodramatic, Jim. You're not suffocating. You're just panting a bit and you have some sweat on your brow.

JIM. I can't do this.

POCAHONTAS *puts down her bags.*

POCAHONTAS. What did you just say?

JIM. I can't do this. I've reached my limit. We all have one. I've reached mine and I just actually can't do this. I'm sorry – I'm very sorry – but... I can no longer continue this relationship. With you. It's over.

RAMONA (*suddenly making for the door*). Okay. I think I might just –

POCAHONTAS. Shut up! Don't fucking move!

RAMONA *stays where she is. Terrified.* POCAHONTAS *stands totally stock-still for two beats. She starts hyperventilating and then shuts her eyes and starts to make a strange, high-pitched whining noise.*

JIM. What are you doing?

The high-pitched whining intensifies.

Stop it.

It gets louder.

Stop it, Pocahontas.

And louder.

Please!

POCAHONTAS *walks over to* JIM's *crustacean collection and snatches up the jar with the hermit crab inside.*

What are you doing?

POCAHONTAS *unscrews the lid.*

What are you doing?

POCAHONTAS *takes out the crab.*

Put it down, Pocahontas.

POCAHONTAS *puts the crab down on the floor.*

Beat.

POCAHONTAS *suddenly grabs the Nespresso machine and slams it down on top of the crab with all her force, letting out a blood-curdling scream.*

Pause.

(*Anguished.*) Why did you do that?

POCAHONTAS. Oh my god is it broken?!

JIM. Yes it is fucking broken!

POCAHONTAS. No, not the crab – the Nespresso machine! Is it broken?!

JIM *is crouched over the hermit crab, devastated.*

JIM. That's my hermit crab. I've had that hermit crab for fifteen years.

POCAHONTAS *continues hyperventilating and gets increasingly upset throughout this speech.*

POCAHONTAS. You are insane. You are a genuinely insane man, Jim. I think you need psychological help. You're so blank. Like a, like an iPhone that won't turn on. It's like you're dead – the most dead alive person I've ever met. Do you know what everyone says about you? You're a perv for going out with me. I'm just a sweet little girl, Jim –

JIM. Please. Please be quiet –

POCAHONTAS. And you're a massive paedo who never talks to anyone and lives in a four hundred-and-fifty-square-foot shithole and murders animals and traps them forever in horrible little jars –

JIM. SHUT. THE FUCK. UP.

POCAHONTAS. Do you mean it? Is this it?

JIM. Yes.

> POCAHONTAS *starts to weep*.

I mean, Jesus, you don't even like me!

POCAHONTAS. I do *like* you actually! I really fucking *like* you. I know you're dull as fuck and fat and you're always blabbing on about crap but you're kind to me, no one has ever been that kind to me. You're lovely!

JIM. What is wrong with you, Pocahontas?

POCAHONTAS. Why does everyone think something's wrong with me?! There's nothing wrong with me! I'm just a nice, normal girl! A nice, normal, delicate, sensitive girl. (*Very quiet and sad and heartfelt.*) I want us to live in a new-build, semi-detached four-bedroom house in a cul-de-sac, Jim. I want black-and-white pictures of New York skylines, I want to go on holiday to Spain and eat giant prawns by the sea, I want to cook you a Beef Wellington when I get home from my job, as a mortgage adviser in the Halifax Bank of Scotland and when we have the baby, I will love her so much and buy her anything she wants. An iPad, a micro-pig, trainers that light up, all the sweets she wants even if her teeth rot. I want a happy, normal life with you, Jim. That's all I want.

JIM. You want a lot.

POCAHONTAS. What's wrong with wanting? I've never had anything I want.

> POCAHONTAS *starts to cry again*.

Is the Nespresso machine broken?

JIM (*peering at the machine*). I think so yes.

> POCAHONTAS *lets out a short wail*. RAMONA *makes for the door once again*.

RAMONA. Right. I really must –

POCAHONTAS (*suddenly pointing at* RAMONA). Do you still think she's pretty?

Beat. JIM *does not respond.*

Do you love her?

Beat. JIM *does not respond.*

POCAHONTAS *suddenly snatches up the broken Nespresso machine and makes for the door. She pauses at* RAMONA *and moves very close to her.*

I can smell death on you.

POCAHONTAS *exits.*

Silence.

JIM *examines the hermit crab. Holds it up to the window then carefully places it on the table.*

He is lost in thought for a moment.

RAMONA. Would you like me to leave?

JIM. I'd like you to stay. Please.

RAMONA *nods.*

RAMONA. Is she genuinely called Pocahontas?

JIM. Yes.

RAMONA. How old is she?

JIM. Nineteen.

Another few beats of silence. RAMONA *inspects the damaged hermit crab on the table.*

RAMONA. That's the hermit crab, isn't it?

JIM. Yup. That you found. When you saw your first selkie.

RAMONA. I saw one again recently. Actually. A selkie.

JIM. Yeah?

RAMONA. Well. I had a dream about one anyway.

JIM. What happened?

RAMONA. It's sort of embarrassing really but you were the selkie and you were all draped in seaweed and wearing tiny pants. Calvin Klein Y-fronts to be precise.

JIM. Definitely me?

RAMONA. Absolutely. And I tried to touch you. Not in a sex way but in an… intrigued way. But as soon as I reached out, I sort of spiralled down into the shingle.

Suddenly RAMONA *lunges at* JIM *and kisses him.* JIM *kisses her powerfully back. They disengage and look at each other.*

Sorry. Just couldn't help myself.

JIM. That's fine. That's absolutely fine.

RAMONA. It feels better, doesn't it?

JIM. Yes.

RAMONA. Good.

JIM. You look so nice.

RAMONA. So do you.

They kiss again.

Eleven

2013.

JIM*'s flat. Later that night. It is in darkness. The stage is empty, then…* RAMONA *creeps on, visibly drunk, wearing one of* JIM*'s shirts. She sits down on the sofa, takes a swig of wine from the bottle, sighs and then settles down to sleep.* POCAHONTAS *silently emerges from the shadows, wearing a floor-length fur coat. Her make-up is all smudged and run down her face.* RAMONA *does not notice her.* POCAHONTAS *watches her for a few beats then…*

POCAHONTAS. Not the greatest lover in the world, is he?

RAMONA *jumps.*

RAMONA. Fucking hell!

POCAHONTAS. Sssh! Don't wake Jim.

RAMONA *remains still. Scared.* POCAHONTAS *moves closer to her.*

How long did he last? I normally endure three, four minutes? It's hard to tell but it's all usually over within the confines of the song 'Clocks' by Coldplay. Are you going to Frankfurt with him?

Beat.

RAMONA. Dunno. Maybe.

POCAHONTAS *looks like she is about to throw a punch at* RAMONA, *but she stops and falls back collapsing into tears.*

Are you okay?

POCAHONTAS. Yeah I'm fucking fantastic! How the fuck are you?

RAMONA. I don't really know.

POCAHONTAS *pulls herself together and focuses on* RAMONA.

POCAHONTAS. How old are you?

RAMONA. Thirty-one.

POCAHONTAS. What do you do? What's your job? Do you work in an office?

RAMONA. Yes.

RAMONA *pours herself a glass of wine.*

POCAHONTAS. What kind of office?

RAMONA. In a lettings agent. It's called Black Katz. And they spell Katz with a K and a Z.

POCAHONTAS. Is it fun?

RAMONA. No.

RAMONA *drains her glass.*

POCAHONTAS. Is that how you can afford to go to Frankfurt, because you have a job in an office?

RAMONA. No I'm just very irresponsible with money.

POCAHONTAS. Do you have your own desk?

RAMONA. Yes.

POCAHONTAS. That's so cool. What about lunch? Do you go to Boots for your lunch?

RAMONA. Sometimes. Or Pret.

POCAHONTAS. Pret? As in Pret A Manger the famous international sandwich-shop chain? Cool. That's so cool. What do you have?

RAMONA. Um, varies I suppose. Sometimes the avocado and crayfish sandwich or occasionally I'll have a falafel wrap.

POCAHONTAS. I'd like to do that. I'd like to have falafel wrap in 'Pret A Manger' on my lunchbreak in my office.

RAMONA. I don't feel that good about it.

POCAHONTAS. Why not?

RAMONA. Because I feel quite sad when I'm there.

RAMONA *pours another glass of wine. Takes a big gulp.*

POCAHONTAS. Are you insane? You feel sad?

RAMONA. Yes I feel sad. My desk faces a wall.

POCAHONTAS. You can't have an office without a wall.

RAMONA *vomits out the following speech whilst intermittently taking huge gulps of wine.*

RAMONA. And there's Blu Tack stains all over it from someone's else's pictures before me and, not only does everyone talk about the girl that was here before me all the time and how amazing she was and how much they miss her but also, I don't have any pictures to put on the wall. I don't even want to put pictures on the wall, why would anyone want to put pictures on the wall? (*Beat.*) Saw Josephine Woodcock the other day. Went to school with her. She put a soiled sanitary towel in my sleeping bag, hadn't seen her for years and I was in the pub, having a quick ploughman's lunch and she tapped me on the shoulder and I turned around and when I saw it was her, I almost vomited, but I managed to keep it in my mouth. I've always fantasised about the moment when I would bump into someone from school years later and I would

be mid-guffaw in an art-house cinema drinking a glass of
Malbec or doing something incredibly cool like ice-skating
really well at Somerset House – you know like doing twirls
and stuff and they would be like, 'Fucking hell, you look
amazing, Ramona, look at you go! Like Torvill only much
more attractive. And your personality is just to die for now!'
But the reality was my face was sweating because I'd just
eaten a really spicy bowl of ramen in Wagamama's –
sometimes I have two lunches if I'm having a bad day – and
my dentist had also just diagnosed me with gingivitis that
morning and so I felt extremely paranoid about my breath and
the build-up of plaque in my receding gums and my shiny face
and I couldn't speak. I literally couldn't speak. For about ten
seconds. And she was just staring at me. Then I said, 'Wow,
cool top. Where did you get your top from?' And she said
'Urban Outfitters,' and I said 'WICKED!' – then I couldn't
think of anything else to say so I just said 'WICKED!' again
and then I bolted. And then I was sick in the street.

Pause.

POCAHONTAS. What a pile of wank. I'd love to have two
lunches. And a job in an office, I applied to be a mortgage
adviser at the Halifax Bank of Scotland. But obviously I won't
get it. Because I don't ever get anything I want.

RAMONA. I don't think being a mortgage adviser would be
that fun to be honest.

POCAHONTAS. It would be fun. You'd get your own desk and
one of those cool headsets.

RAMONA. I really think there are more exciting things to be
than a mortgage adviser.

POCAHONTAS. Like what? I can't think of anything that
could possibly be better than being a mortgage adviser. Tell
me what?

RAMONA *thinks. Drinks more wine.*

RAMONA. Like you could go travelling! I always wanted to
travel. You could go abroad – go to Burma! Because it's
opening up now, you know?

POCAHONTAS. Where's Burma?

RAMONA. It's um… I think it's nearish south-east Asia, type thing.

POCAHONTAS. What would I do in Burma?

RAMONA. I don't know really. Just travel. And look around Burma? Or South America? There's like an *amazing* orang-utan rehabilitation sanctuary there –

POCAHONTAS. I hate orang-utans.

RAMONA. Fair enough. What about going to London? London's fun. Loads going on in London. You could open a pop-up calzone stall! I've always wanted to do that.

POCAHONTAS. What's a calzone?

RAMONA. It's an oven-baked folded pizza.

POCAHONTAS. Why the fuck would you fold a pizza?

RAMONA. Dunno really. It's just what you do. Fold a pizza.

Beat. POCAHONTAS *appraises* RAMONA.

POCAHONTAS. I think you're a very weird person. And I don't think you're a very nice person. I know most people think I'm stupid and pointless and everything but I know things and see things that other people don't – like I can see you are not a nice person and you don't deserve Jim and I wish you hadn't come here because you've ruined everything and you just ruin things, don't you? You just run around ruining things for other people and you just think about yourself and you don't even realise that you ruin things because you're so blind to everything around you, because you're such a shit person.

Beat.

RAMONA. Yeah. Not a bad analysis, to be fair.

RAMONA *pours another glass of wine.*

POCAHONTAS. I also think you're a borderline alcoholic.

RAMONA. Again. Very well observed. Sometimes I worry about that too. Although I don't start before six so I'm probably just normal.

POCAHONTAS. Do you like my coat?

RAMONA. It's... lovely yes.

POCAHONTAS. Thank you. It's made of sixteen and a half foxes. I bought it on eBay using my mum's credit card because I thought it might make me happy but it only made me feel happy for approximately twenty-nine minutes and then I felt sad again and then my mum found out I had used her credit card and she cut the sleeves off all my pyjamas.

Beat. POCAHONTAS *takes her coat off to reveal she is wearing sleeveless pyjamas.*

She cut the sleeves off all my pyjamas! Why would she do that? I love my pyjamas! Can I stay the night?

RAMONA. It's not really up to me.

POCAHONTAS. But I can't go back home.

RAMONA. Why not?

POCAHONTAS. I think I might die there. I think I might explode. I think something really bad might happen.

RAMONA *has no idea what to do.* POCAHONTAS *makes to go then pauses.*

He's not always that nice, you know. He's a bit like one of those rescue dogs. You feel sorry for it because it looks so sad and pathetic and ugly and you spend ages being kind to it and stroking it and feeding it and loving it and then it goes and bites you and you sort of don't mind because you know it's fucked up.

POCAHONTAS *exits.* RAMONA *drains the wine. She begins to retch, grabs a nearby spider plant and vomits into it.*

Twelve

2013.

The morning after. RAMONA *is asleep on the sofa.* JIM *enters. He watches* RAMONA *for a few beats and then slowly creeps towards her. He leans in and does the seal bark.*

JIM. Ow! Ow! Ow!

RAMONA. What the fuck?!

JIM. Sorry.

RAMONA. Fuck!

JIM. Sorry. I was doing the seal bark?

RAMONA. The what?

JIM. The um seal bark? Remember the seal bark? When we were... In my caravan we –

RAMONA. Oh yes. Sorry yes, yes I do remember that.

JIM. Were you um... uncomfortable upstairs?

RAMONA. Yes. Sorry I was a bit... hot. So came downstairs.

JIM. Don't blame ya! My duvet is fourteen-point-five tog so it is pretty fucking hot. Ha! (*Beat.*) Now of course you can get those fabulous multi-seasonal duvets which you can simply adjust according to the um... To the um –

RAMONA. Season?

JIM. Exactly. Yes.

RAMONA. I vomited in your spider plant.

    Beat. JIM *stiffens.*

JIM. What?

RAMONA. I'm really sorry but I vomited into your spider plant.

JIM. My spider plant?

RAMONA. Yes. Sorry.

    JIM *struggles to contain his anguish.*

JIM. Why did you do that?

RAMONA. I didn't mean to – I just grabbed it because it was the closest contraption –

JIM. Oh dear.

RAMONA. I'm sorry.

JIM. No that's okay. That's fine. (*Slight pause.*) Which one?

RAMONA. What –

JIM. Which one? Which spider plant?

RAMONA. Um –

JIM. Was it the big one? (*Pointing at a large, lustrous spider plant.*) That one there?

RAMONA. Yes.

JIM *winces, picks up the spider plant and peers into the pot, dismayed.*

JIM. Oh... there's quite a lot, isn't there?

RAMONA. I know, it was a couple of bouts. I really am sorry. I'll buy you a new one.

JIM *takes a deep breath and exhales. A beat.*

JIM. Oh no need, no need. Not a big deal. At all. It's fine. It's absolutely fine.

Pause.

But I did like that one though. I did really, really like that one. That one was my favourite, the mother plant. She was the mother to all my babies.

RAMONA. I mean um... I'm no gardener but will the vomit act a bit like fertiliser?

JIM. Fertiliser? No. Nope it definitely will not act like a fertiliser, Ramona. In fact the acid in your vomit will undoubtedly kill it. (*Beat.*) But that's okay.

RAMONA. I really am sorry.

JIM. No need to be sorry.

RAMONA. Okay.

JIM *sits on the sofa with his head in his hands. Pause.*
RAMONA *is unsure what to do. She looks towards the door.*
JIM *suddenly stands up.*

JIM. Sorry… I honestly don't give a shit about the spider plant.
I'm fine now. I'm fine. I'm absolutely fine. I'm sorry. (*Beat.*)
But it was a shit thing to do, I think you can see that, and I
was like, where is she? I thought she was lying beside me, oh
no, she's decided to – doesn't matter but – vom on my best
pot plant. Ha! But let's just forget it. It's fine. I'm sorry.

Pause. JIM *eyes* RAMONA *intensely. He moves towards her.*

You look beautiful.

RAMONA. Do I? I don't feel very beautiful.

JIM. No honestly. Really, really, really fucking beautiful.

RAMONA *laughs nervously.*

(*Offended.*) Why are you laughing?

RAMONA. No, I was just – I'm not. Thank you.

JIM *suddenly kisses* RAMONA *urgently. She remains quite
rigid but doesn't stop him. He stops kissing her and looks
straight in her eyes.*

JIM. It feels good. Doesn't it? This. Us.

RAMONA…. Yes.

JIM. I feel good about it, I feel really good about it, do you feel
good about it?

RAMONA. Um… Quite good. I suppose. But also I feel…
Quite sad.

JIM. Sad? Why do you feel sad? This is amazing. Last night
was amazing. Wasn't it?

RAMONA. Yes. (*Beat.*) I had had a lot of wine though. Too
much wine as bloody per. Ha!

JIM. What are you saying?

RAMONA. Just saying I got pissed, I'm just having a laugh.

JIM. No, but what are you actually saying?

RAMONA. Nothing. Just saying I was drunk. Too much to drink. I drink too much.

JIM. What are you actually saying though?

RAMONA. I'm not saying anything.

Beat.

JIM. You don't want to go home, do you?

RAMONA. I don't know.

JIM. Well, it's quite simple, isn't it? You either want to go home or you don't.

RAMONA. I'm just not sure me coming to Frankfurt is… Is the best idea.

Beat.

JIM. Why?

RAMONA. Because –

JIM. Because what? Can you just actually say what you're trying to say?

RAMONA *suddenly makes for the door.*

RAMONA. I'm sorry but I really think I should just go.

JIM *runs ahead and stands in front of the door.* RAMONA *looks at him. He stares back. Not moving. Pause.*

JIM. Would you like a boiled egg, Ramona?

RAMONA. Um. No thank you.

JIM. Stay and have a boiled egg.

RAMONA. I don't want one.

JIM. Please just have a boiled fucking egg.

Beat.

RAMONA. Can I get past?

JIM. I'm not sure you can.

RAMONA. Why not?

JIM. Just stay. It'll be nice.

Slight pause. RAMONA *is still.*

Please. Stay. Eat an egg – or don't eat an egg. But just stay.
And let's just, fucking – Jesus, can we not just get along? So
this trip's not really awkward – I mean, I don't want to be
sitting on the flight and you're all –

RAMONA. I can't come to Frankfurt with you, Jim. Obviously
I can't. I mean, I don't even know you.

JIM. What?

RAMONA. I don't know you.

JIM. You do.

RAMONA. I don't. You're a stranger. We're strangers. So we
just have to accept the fact that, in the past, someone told a lie
to someone else and that we as people, in truth, aren't really
connected any more. I'm not sure we even like each other
really and genuinely why would I want to come to a fucking
fish conference or whatever it is? In Frankfurt? I mean, isn't
Frankfurt quite shit?

JIM *tries hard to remain calm.*

JIM. Why are you trying to make me angry?

RAMONA. I'm not.

JIM. Is that what you want?

RAMONA. No.

JIM. Would you like me to shout at you? Would that make you
feel better? Would you like me to shout at you and tell you
how terrible you are and tell you that you've completely
fucked up my life but ultimately I'm *so* glad you came all the
way here and told me the truth because that's definitely made
it all better? Would that make you feel good?

RAMONA. No it wouldn't.

JIM. You have no idea what you do to people, do you? You
have no idea the effect you have on the environment around
you. You just slither into people's lives, vomit all over their
spider plants and fuck off.

Pause. JIM *smiles sardonically and nods.*

'Isn't Frankfurt quite shit?' Ha! Isn't Frankfurt quite shit? Haha. No. Frankfurt is not fucking shit, Ramona.

As he speaks, JIM *starts walking towards* RAMONA, *slowly. As he does, she backs away. He speaks calmly as he moves towards her.*

Frankfurt is fabulous. Frankfurt is the third largest city in Germany, a cosmopolitan melting pot and home to the Annual World Crustacean Congress 2013. Can you imagine going to a congress specifically to celebrate crustacea? Where crustacean biologists from over fifteen countries come together to discuss their crustacean-based research? Where there's a whole lecture dedicated purely to the Japanese spider crabs? I'm going to be meeting Larry frigging Turbine, for crying out loud! Larry Turbine! The most respected taxonomist in California. He knows everything there is to know about crustacea! Because people just don't understand do they? Just how incredible, just how joyful a crustacean really is and... Can I have a hug?

RAMONA *embraces* JIM *tightly for a few beats. Then* JIM *suddenly springs back.*

This is embarrassing. Ha! What am I doing? I don't know what I'm doing, what am I doing? I honestly have absolutely no idea what I'm doing. (*Picks up the spider plant again, suddenly positive.*) You know I think I can maybe just give this a quick rinse under the tap, repot it, got some compost somewhere. Probably be absolutely fine...

RAMONA. Jim, I'm sorry, I honestly am.

JIM. Don't be sorry. Sorry is useless.

Pause.

(*Bright.*) Are you sure you wouldn't like an egg? You could just stay, eat an egg and then go.

RAMONA. No. I... I really have to get back.

JIM. I don't know what to do when you're gone is the thing. I have absolutely no idea what I'm going to do.

Beat.

RAMONA. Jim, I really think you need to get some –

JIM. Do you like the song 'Clocks' by Coldplay?

RAMONA. It's… good yes – I like it.

JIM. Me too. I love it. It's a fantastic track.

JIM *just stands still, thinking.* RAMONA *watches him. A couple of beats of silence.*

I wanted to do that to him anyway, you know.

Pause.

What I did to Darren. I'd thought about it so many times. It felt good.

Pause.

I mean, I know that's not quite right. I know that sounds a bit odd. When I say it out loud.

Pause.

Can you please leave now? I really, really, really want you to leave.

RAMONA. Do you think you'll be okay?

JIM. Oh yes.

RAMONA. I really am sorry about your plant, and…

JIM. Not a problem at all. It's just a plant. I'll buy a new one.

RAMONA *leaves.* JIM *sits down. He looks straight ahead.*

Thirteen

1998.

The Beach. Night. JIM (*seventeen*) *stands very still, looking straight ahead. He has blood on his face and hands. A few beats.* RAMONA (*sixteen*) *suddenly runs on, out of breath. She stops when she sees him.*

RAMONA. Oh dear.

Beat.

JIM. What?

RAMONA. You've got…

JIM. What?

RAMONA. On your face. There's like… quite a lot of… blood. On your face.

JIM touches his face. Looks blankly at the blood on his hand. He doesn't react.

Beat.

Are you worried?

JIM. No. Are you worried?

RAMONA. No.

JIM. Cool.

Beat.

RAMONA. So. What um… What exactly did you… What did you do to him?

JIM. Doesn't matter.

RAMONA. Okay. That's fine. That's okay. That's fine. That's totally fine.

RAMONA gathers herself. Beat.

JIM. But it was the right thing to do, wasn't it?

RAMONA. Oh yes. Absolutely.

JIM. Good.

RAMONA. Absolutely yes.

JIM. Good.

RAMONA. I mean, I don't know exactly what you did. But in theory, yes. Absolutely fine.

JIM. Cool.

RAMONA. Cool.

JIM. Cool.

RAMONA. Good.

JIM. Good.

Beat. JIM *turns to* RAMONA.

I like you, Ramona. Even though you're massively flawed.

RAMONA. I like you too. Even though I also think you're massively flawed.

Beat.

JIM. Brilliant.

RAMONA. Cool.

JIM. Yeah.

Slight pause.

RAMONA. It definitely will be alright, won't it?

JIM. Oh yes.

RAMONA. Good.

JIM. I think you're amazing.

RAMONA. I don't give a shit what you think about me.

JIM. Oh.

RAMONA. In a good way. Does that sound stupid?

JIM. No.

RAMONA. I feel like I can be ugly and stupid and tell you bad jokes and have halitosis breath and small boobs and an extra-long middle toe but you'll still actually like me?

JIM. I think, apart from my mum, you're probably the best person I've ever met.

RAMONA. I prefer you to my mum. And my chinchilla.

JIM. When I get out, Ramona, I'm going to whisk you off to the pine-clad island of Paxos, without your slut of a mother and we'll rescue all the cats and eat all the olives until we're sick and then we'll have loads of babies and shitloads of houses all across the world because I'll be like some genius professor and you'll be like – what do you wanna be?

RAMONA. I'll be a writer of popular fiction but also have a cat rescue centre on the side?

JIM. Perfect! And when we die which will probably be around the age of ninety-eight, we'll die spooning –

RAMONA. In a four-poster mahogany bed with a cool breeze wafting over us from an open window!

JIM. I was just gonna say that!

RAMONA. Were you?

JIM. Yes.

RAMONA. Wow. That's so specific. But cool.

JIM. I think we basically have the same brain.

RAMONA. I think we are basically one person.

The sound of police sirens in the distance.

JIM. I should go.

JIM *makes to leave.*

RAMONA. Wait! Jim, I –

A beat.

JIM. What?

RAMONA *lunges at* JIM *and kisses him.*

RAMONA. Just wanted to give you a farewell snog.

JIM. Lovely. Well. Will you write to me?

RAMONA. Yes. I'll write to you.

JIM. Okay. I'd like that.

RAMONA. Goodbye, Jim.

JIM. Goodbye, Ramona.

JIM *walks away.* RAMONA *watches him. She fidgets.*

Epilogue

RAMONA (*thirty-one*) *stands alone onstage*.

RAMONA. Everything is black.

Beat.

And all the tiny shards of shingle, all the minute pebbles and bits of shell dig into my flesh and fill my mouth and smother my eyeballs and I can't breathe or move. And at first I panic and struggle… But then I stop and I stay very still and I let myself melt into the ground and I feel like I'm made of sand too and I can just about still hear the sea lapping at the edges of the beach and finally I wake up. I'm in my bed and it's so dark and cold and I know straight away there is something next to me, with a tail and a wet, whiskery nose. I move closer to it, put my arms around it and we spoon and I can smell the sea on his damp back and I let my fingers run through the seaweed in his hair and then suddenly we are standing up and Enya Patricia Brennan's sweet, dulcet voice is filling the room…

Enya's 'Orinoco Flow' begins to swell and gets louder and louder. RAMONA *dances with the seal.*

And we are dancing round and round and round, faster and faster and faster until my head is spinning and the room is full of stars – so many exploding stars – and then we collapse onto the floor in a puddle of flesh and blubber and seaweed. And I blink. And when I open my eyes again… he's gone.

A Nick Hern Book

Ramona Tells Jim first published in Great Britain in 2017 as a paperback original by Nick Hern Books Limited, The Glasshouse, 49a Goldhawk Road, London W12 8QP, in association with the Bush Theatre, London

Ramona Tells Jim copyright © 2017 Sophie Wu

Sophie Wu has asserted her moral right to be identified as the author of this work

Front cover image: Studio Doug

Designed and typeset by Nick Hern Books, London
Printed in Great Britain by Mimeo Ltd, Huntingdon, Cambridgeshire PE29 6XX

A CIP catalogue record for this book is available from the British Library

ISBN 978 1 84842 670 2

Woodland
CARBON
www.woodlandcarbon.co.uk
NICK HERN BOOKS
Printed on Carbon Captured paper